$7.00

+ T

Conrad

A KING'S LESSONS
IN   STATECRAFT

LOUIS XIV
(1638–1715)

From an Engraving by Achille Ouvré

After a Pastel by NANTEUIL

A KING'S LESSONS IN STATECRAFT: LOUIS XIV : LETTERS TO HIS HEIRS WITH INTRODUCTION AND NOTES *by* JEAN LONGNON

TRANSLATED BY
HERBERT WILSON

KENNIKAT PRESS
Port Washington, N. Y./London

A KING'S LESSONS IN STATECRAFT

First published in 1924
Reissued in 1970 by Kennikat Press
Library of Congress Catalog Card No: 77-110913
SBN 8046-0895-4 *1-26-93*

Manufactured by Taylor Publishing Company   Dallas, Texas

CONTENTS

INTRODUCTION

ONE EVENING IN THE YEAR 1714, Louis XIV
sent the Maréchal de Noailles to his private
study to fetch some papers lying in the
drawers, and began burning them one by one. He had
already burnt a portion of them concerning the reputation of various high personages when the Maréchal
earnestly begged him to entrust the rest to his safe keeping.
These papers, which de Noailles placed in the King's
Library subsequently in 1749, had all been written
by Louis XIV, and consisted of his military notes,
his journal, and his memoirs.

Recollections of a far distant period very different
from his latter years, lost illusions, and the follies of
youth, were doubtless all that his work as a writer
represented in the eyes of the aged king—matters
which for him were now no longer anything but vanity.
What a far cry from the sovereign of seventy-six
tried by adversity, by the misery of his people, and by
domestic losses, to the young hero of twenty-eight
who, amid the glamour of his victories in Flanders
and Franche-Comté, and in the opening glory of a
reign rendered illustrious by Literature and Art, was
beginning to write his Memoirs !

In 1666, it was five years since Louis XIV, on the death
of Mazarin, had taken the exercise of power into his
own hands, and had entered into all the details of public

affairs. He had restored the kingdom from the anarchy into which the Fronde had plunged it, and its finances from the lamentable state in which the wasteful administration of Fouquet had left them ; he had driven the English from Dunkerque, had upheld the *prestige* of France at the Pontifical Court, had swept the Mediterranean of the pirates which were infesting it, had disputed the sovereignty of the sea with the English and Dutch, and by sending help to Hungary had made his power felt by the Emperor, his ally of a day, as much as by the Turks whom he had contributed to defeat. He had created the Académie des Inscriptions et Médailles and the Académie des Sciences, and had organised the Académie de Peinture et de Sculpture ; the magnificent *fêtes* of the *Plaisirs de l'Ile Enchantée* had been held on the newly made lawns at Versailles by the side of which the new palace was beginning ; *Tartuffe* had been played before the Court, and *Alexandre* had been produced in homage of a young king eager for glory and love.

Amid this epic atmosphere Louis XIV took in hand the setting down in writing of the principal events of his reign—a remarkable undertaking on the part of a man whose literary education had been neglected, but who, in the words of Saint-Simon, had " a mind able to mould, polish, and refine itself, and to learn from others, without copying them, and without effort." It was something new in a sovereign, but must have been suggested to him by Sully's *Economies Royales* and the *Testament Politique* of Richelieu. Becoming in 1661 his own Prime Minister, Louis XIV had a similar idea of undertaking a work for his own justification and instruction, as the great Ministers before him had in regard to his predecessors. Has he not written at the very beginning of his Memoirs that kings " owe, as it were, a public account of their actions to the whole world and to all succeeding centuries " ?

Louis XIV liked to verify the details of public affairs, and to give his personal and considered advice on all that concerned his own government or *prestige*. On the margin of an estimate prepared by Le Brun for Versailles, he objected " entirely childish throughout," and himself drew up a *Manière de voir le jardin de Versailles* for the benefit of august visitors. It was not a question of literary vanity with him, but a self-imposed work of reflection, a consciousness of his great *rôle*, and a desire to justify his actions by reason.

Louis XIV conceived the idea of giving an account of his actions at the outset of his taking over the reins in 1661. Mazarin on his death-bed had left him a programme of government ; immediately after his death the King had " the items drawn out at great length " by his secretary Rose, and from that time he ordered to be noted down in writing the business of his Council ; these written notes, according to Monsieur J. de Boislisle, who has edited them, " must have been in his mind, and gave rise to the Annals of personal government."

Colbert, who was happy to encourage this labour of love which he admired in his master, made himself his literary collaborator. Basing it on the *Memoriaux du Conseil*, he undertook a " diary of all that passed, written up every week so as to be of use for the King's journal." He worked for some time on the narrative of Louis XIV, even writing with his own hand ten or twenty pages of the *Mémoire pour l'Instruction du Dauphin*, which, later on, was to serve as material for the Memoirs of 1661. But in 1665, overtaxed by the administration of public affairs, he was obliged to give up his collaboration.

In 1666, therefore, Louis XIV took up the work again. At the beginning of the year he began to make notes himself, month by month and almost day by day, of all the matters wherein he was earnestly busying himself. These sheets in the King's handwriting, which have been preserved with the Memoirs, only contain brief notes, such as : " The negotiations with England. The different incidents connected therewith. What I have done to preserve peace, etc." As the King wrote on one of these sheets, they are simply " Notes pour servir aux Mémoires."

In the inception of this work, and during its continuation, Louis XIV dictated after a fashion to one of his secretaries the kind of development he wished to be given to his own written sheets. " From Saturday, the twenty-sixth of June," the secretary wrote, " His Majesty explained the matter which follows, from two small sheets written on both sides." The King began giving this new form to his *souvenirs* on the 14th February, and on that day dealt with matters in the month of January and the first days of February. The commentary thus follows hard on the course of events. Necessarily, he gave a disjointed narrative. But already he was trying to obtain a proper perspective, and to give it a loftier point of view. In this Journal, as the historian Dreyss called it, we come across reasoned reflections, the subject of which had already been indicated by a word in the sheets written by the King, and is to be found more fully drawn out in the Memoirs. They contain all the essentials of the royal work, and as they came from the mouth of the King himself.

Whose was the pen, then, which wrote this " spoken "

Journal, if we may so call it, associating himself thus closely in the work of the King ? It appears that it was sometimes one and sometimes several secretaries. " The King told me," we generally find ; but sometimes, " The King said to us." These collaborators were doubtless the King's readers ; and we shall definitely come across one of them. The Journal shows them to be conscientiously doing their work. " I must remind the King to explain to me . . ." one of them wrote. And this remark also shows that the pages of the Journal were still only notes, but this time for the use of the secretary.

Many months passed during which Louis XIV continued his two-fold work of making notes and dictating. Then, after the short campaigns in Flanders and Franche-Comté, came leisure with the Treaty of Aix-la-Chapelle. This was doubtless the moment, during the spring of 1668, when Louis XIV began to give a definite shape to his Memoirs for a definite end.

The Dauphin was just seven years old. The King, who had a natural love for children and cherished his own with unremitting affection, was concerned as regards his education. While in Flanders and Franche-Comté, he corresponded on this matter with the governess, the Maréchale de la Motte, and in the midst of his pre-occupations and his human ideals, his love of good sense and courtesy stands out ; he wishes the Dauphin to be made *sage et modéré* ; he hopes that he will become *honnête homme*. It was just at this time when the Dauphin was to leave the tutelage of women for that of men, his pupillage under Madame de la Motte for that of Montausier, that Louis XIV began to write his Memoirs for the instruction of his son in politics.

The Dauphin had had Périgny for his tutor for three

years, a man of an upright and enlightened character who is only remembered to-day because, according to Cardinal de Bausset, he was succeeded by Bossuet. His appointment as tutor dated from September 1666, but he had already been fulfilling that office for over a year while acting as the King's Reader. And it was this man who was chosen by Louis XIV to collaborate in his Memoirs when Colbert was compelled to relinquish the work.

For a long time this collaboration had been attributed to Pellisson, although the latter only revised a portion of the Memoirs. The part played by Périgny was only discovered by the historian Dreyss in 1860, and the matter is no longer in doubt. An examination of the original texts, and a comparison of the manuscripts in the Bibliothèque with two little notes in the handwriting of Périgny in which all the characters, even the most distinctive, correspond (as we have ourselves been able to verify), demonstrate that the greater part of the work on the Memoirs is certainly due to him. In addition, he had often taken down in writing the Journal dictated by the King.

Notwithstanding, the original composition of the Memoirs still does not appear to have been the work of Périgny ; the manuscripts are in a handwriting which was not his but that of the trusty Rose, the secretary who had consigned Mazarin's instructions to writing.

With the assistance of a secretary, possibly Rose at first, and Périgny subsequently, Louis XIV began therefore, in 1668, the serious compilation of his Memoirs in the form of Instructions for the young Dauphin. He worked on the notes contained in the sheets written in his own handwriting, and in the Journal. He began with the year 1666 with the view of bringing it up to the time of writing. In the end, in order to give a more complete account, he decided to go back to the beginnings of his personal government by relating, in a kind of introduction, the events of the years 1661 to 1665, with the aid of the notes put together by Colbert.

Louis XIV carried this out in 1669 or 1670, and Périgny was still acting as his secretary at the commencement of the work. But in September 1670 he died, and Bossuet succeeded him as tutor to the Dauphin, and Pellisson took his place with the King on the work of the Memoirs. He took in hand the first portion, on the years 1661 and 1662, which had been already compiled, and re-edited it, as is shown by the manuscripts received by the Bibliothèque from the Maréchal de Noailles.

In the spring of 1672 war started again—in Holland this time. The King, who was at the head of his army, relinquished his Memoirs, but only provisionally as it appears, for he continued to make notes, this time connected with military questions, and after the Treaty of Nimègue in 1679 he still wrote political reflections in his own hand, of which a fragment has been preserved, and to which the title, *Réflexions sur le Métier de Roi*, has been given. But in 1679 the Dauphin had become a man, and there could no longer be any question of instructions ; he was directly taking his part in the government. The Memoirs were therefore discontinued. Only two portions of this great disconnected undertaking were realised—the years 1666 to 1668, written at the time, and the years 1661 and 1662 compiled nearly ten years after the events.

We find several people of differing degrees of importance in the immediate *entourage* of Louis XIV working with him on the Memoirs—Colbert, Périgny, Pellisson, and a secretary, possibly Rose. What part did each of them play, and what part was reserved to the King? It is always a delicate matter to decide the proper share in any work which falls to the actual writer and to the official secretaries who translate the commands of a great personage into writing. Practically speaking, we find the King first noting down events in his own hand and reflections thereon ; then dictating a succinct development of these notes and finally causing the definite text of the Memoirs to be written out by a secretary. We even find in this text differences in methods of rendering and in style, according to whether Périgny or Pellisson was acting as secretary. The material collaboration of Louis XIV thus appears to be diminishing as it goes on. But we must note this : the King may seem to be vanishing, but he was always on the spot and taking an active part.

Let us take, for example, the last part of the Memoirs to be written out and recast, namely, the revision made by Pellisson of the year 1661. On the margin of the manuscript in the Bibliothèque Nationale we see three kinds of annotation, one in ink, one in blue pencil, and one in black pencil. The two first are those made by Pellisson ; the last are by Louis XIV. As a rule, the King marked with a cross the passages to be remodelled, and gave instructions by word of mouth what correction to make, as Pellisson informs us in a marginal note : " The King improved this passage ; I could not well remember his exact phrases, and I may have omitted other things besides." Sometimes the King himself altered what had been written, as, for example, in the passage wherein the original text spoke of the liberty he permitted to all to speak to him of outside affairs at all times ; he added with his pencil the following remark, which is in accordance with one of his habitual characteristics : ". . . with the exception of foreign ministers, who sometimes find too favourable opportunities in the familiarity allowed to them either to obtain, or to discover something."

Similar corrections in the hand of Louis XIV are noticeable, not only in the account of the years 1661 and 1662, but also in that of the years 1666 to 1668. The King, therefore, carefully supervised the work, and intervened in the most trivial details. In one case he corrected the termination of a word ; *passagers* was changed to *passages* in his handwriting. In another, he gave a correction in a matter of style ; Pellisson had written : ". . . un certain détail où ni nos occupations ni notre dignité même nous permettent pas de descendre " ; the King's pencil came into play, and the sentence was shortened into : ". . . où nos occupations et notre dignité même ne nous permettent pas de descendre."

All this is enlightening as to the way in which the work of the Memoirs was done. The secretary composed the text from the notes written on sheets in the King's hand, and from the Journal dictated by him. But at his elbow was the King who explained, corrected, and developed his thought. The secretary constantly referred to him : " I must remind the King to explain to me . . . " Périgny notes ; and Pellisson says of his revision of the year 1661 : " Substantially, this is only a rough draft which will be completed when the intention of His Majesty has been thoroughly grasped." Are we to understand that certain reflections, which have been added in Pellisson's rendering, may have come from some other hand than that of Louis XIV ? Besides representing his mind exactly, most of them would have seemed to be very presumptuous hints offered to the King if they had been actually made by his secretary. The number of successive renderings made of one portion alone shows how much the matter was threshed out between Louis XIV and those who held the pen, and what an important place it held in the King's thoughts.

Throughout the development of the work we notice a well-defined uniformity. The narrative, the reflections, and the sheets in the King's hand consisting of hasty notes, all contain in the first place the material of the Memoirs which we find again in greater detail in the Journal dictated by him, and its full development in the finished rendering. And if the portion written by Périgny differs slightly in form from Pellisson's revision, the essential character and spirit of the two is the same ; it bears the royal impress.

How could it be otherwise ? When he entrusted any work to a secretary Louis XIV did not abdicate his personality or authority. In this connection Sainte-Beuve recalls the remark of the King to Brienne concerning some letters patent drawn up by Arnauld d'Andilly : " Do them over again, and make me speak like a King and not like a Jansenist." And the author of the *Lundis* adds : " This *royal note* Louis XIV imposed accordingly upon Périgny and Pellisson, and they took pains to observe it in the compilation he entrusted to them ; and it is this special mark we have to trace and recognise to-day, without seeking to exalt unduly this or that secretary." In spite of certain unavoidable characteristics the personality of the secretaries effaces itself ; the style all through the revisions becomes more impersonal ; it follows the King's mode of thought, and undoubtedly often reproduces his manner of expression in the dictated Journal, in his spoken explanations, and in his correction of the manuscript. It is true that subsequent writings in the King's own hand, such as *Le Projet de Harangue*, written in 1710, which is included in this book, show greater loftiness in a simpler form. But Sallier, a learned critic of the eighteenth century thought he discovered the King's style running through entire pages in the Memoirs. In reality, the latter truly show the handiwork of Louis XIV, the work of his brain as expressed, revised, and re-polished by his attentive labours, and present a faithful and curious reflection of the great King.

Colbert's part in the Memoirs consists more especially in the preparation of the first portion—the picture of France and Europe in the year 1661, and the hasty glance over the finances between the years 1661 and 1665. Notes in the hand of the minister, which have been preserved, formed without any doubt material which was used by the editors of the Memoirs. His historical notes, however, do not appear to have been utilised in their entirety, for we find here and there greater exactness in them than in the work done by the King. We know, too, that Colbert gave up his connection with the Memoirs just when the compilation really began.

Périgny was the chief collaborator with the King. It was he who frequently wrote down the Journal, who corrected and revised the Memoirs for the years 1666 to 1668, and beyond a doubt drew up the years dealing with 1661 and 1662. When working on the former renderings—such as for the years 1666 to 1668, he introduced order and clearness into a narrative that was rather fragmentary and dragging. As compared with Pellisson's revision, the Memoirs, as re-edited by Périgny, run more easily. The Dauphin's tutor has thus somewhat impressed his own qualities on the King's work.

Pellisson, who for a long time was credited with the Memoirs of Louis XIV, only revised the years 1661 and 1662. He did this with care, freely remodelling them, and not hesitating to suggest additions and corrections to the King. He notes : " Two things seem to have been forgotten, namely, the increase in the number of troops and also the increase of the valuable furniture belonging to the crown, precious stones, etc." He confides to Louis XIV his difficulties and misgivings as a secretary in rendering faithfully the royal thoughts : " Will the King, if it so please him, have the goodness to tell me if I have put in too many or too few reflections and counsels to suit his purpose ? From what I have seen I am persuaded that it is advisable to put . . . I have laid stress on the need of his giving his mind to it, which Monseigneur appears to require most ; but substantially, this is only a rough draft which will be completed when the intention of His Majesty has been thoroughly grasped, although there is no one, without exception, who need have any fear when writing for him."

Pellisson gives a fuller rendering to the text of the Memoirs, more complete pictures, more finished portraits, and more sententious reflections. He employs an eloquent and pompous style which sometimes makes us regret the ease of Périgny, but which is not lacking in majesty, although this comes more naturally from Louis XIV.

There were other collaborators besides—those who with Périgny wrote out the Journal at the King's dictation, and the one who drew up the first versions of the years 1666 to 1668 in a fine, large, and free hand, doubtless some secretary, like Rose, whose handwriting resembled in a striking manner that of the King. This secretary was content to follow closely in his rendering the Journal dictated by the King. Possibly he may only have held the pen like the others who had collaborated in the Journal. This point is very obscure, as though to leave to the King's own handiwork the greater part of the Memoirs.

The historical importance of the events dealt with in the Memoirs should not be lost sight of. The first portion comprises the years 1661 and 1662 ; it was just when Louis XIV began to govern by himself, after the death of Mazarin. The Fronde had left the King's authority weakened, and Fouquet's administration had involved the finances. Louis restored the royal authority, rehabilitated the finances with the aid of Colbert, curbed the pretensions of the Parliaments, and upheld the *prestige* of France abroad.

In the first portion home affairs are dealt with more especially. But in the second, extending from 1666 to 1668, foreign affairs, war, and diplomacy, held the first place. " In the first portion of these Memoirs," Louis XIV says in a rendering which was afterwards abandoned, " I have made known to you how I conducted myself in peace time, and in the second I claim to show you what I did during the war. In the former, I have endeavoured to enlighten you as to the way in which a wise prince may profit from the public tranquillity ; in the latter, I shall instruct you how he should provide for every eventuality which the clash of arms produces."

The year 1666 opened upon a two-fold prospect of war. The King of Spain had just died, and Louis counted greatly upon gaining some advantage in Flanders therefrom ; on the other hand, England had declared war upon Holland with whom the King had recently made an alliance in order to further his designs in Flanders and found himself faced with the necessity of fulfilling his engagements. After hesitating whether he should wage the two wars on both fronts he decided to settle the dispute with England in a rapid campaign which occupied the year 1666, and after the conclusion of peace he turned his armies against Spain, invaded Flanders, which he conquered during the three summer months of 1667, then Franche-Comté, of which he made himself master in seventeen days, and finally on the 2nd May 1668 concluded the Treaty of Aix-la-Chapelle which gave us Flanders.

The interest of the Memoirs does not consist, however, so much in the events themselves, on which we are informed from many other more precise and sometimes more accurate sources, as in the political reflections which these events suggested. The original and true title of Louis XIV's work is *Instructions* and not *Memoires*.

In the *Panégyrique* which he read to the Académie on 3rd February 1671, Pellisson described the Memoirs of Louis XIV as containing " The secret of royalty, and the ever-enduring lessons of what should be avoided and what pursued "—lessons founded upon experience, based upon facts, and given in conformity with the occasion. Understood in this way, advice is less unfruitful and more striking than mere maxims ; the young boy could find interest in the narrative and follow more readily the reflections suggested by it ; he was enabled to grasp cause and effect in the realm of politics, and to accustom himself to reflect on events.

This work was not only serviceable to the Dauphin, but it assisted the King. It was of far greater value to him ; it enabled him to draw upon his own experience of governing, to ponder more deeply and carefully over what he had seen, and to set forth and define the political views which such reflections suggested. Did he not write in these same Memoirs : " The mind brings to fruition its own thoughts by giving them the light of day, whereas before it held them in confusion, undeveloped, and rough-hewn " ? This work of compilation was his opportunity of bringing his thoughts to fruition by giving them expression. He derived pleasure from it as well, happy in giving play to good common sense, and to that faculty for generalisation which, with its good and bad qualities, is very much a national characteristic.

It is not possible to sum up all the train of reflections which arose from the circumstances contained in the narrative. All we can do is to mention a few characteristics. The special dominating note running through the political counsel of Louis XIV, and the one which in his view should inspire the sovereign, was the welfare of the kingdom and the interests of France. This point of view often recurs in his Memoirs. We find it in the most insignificant details. The text of the Memoirs for 1667, when dealing with the affairs of Poland, says : " What touched me most was the consideration that one rarely finds an opportunity of presenting any one with a crown," and Louis XIV added in his own hand : "... *et de l'assurer à la France.*"

In the eyes of Louis XIV the interests of France were identified with those of the sovereign. " The interests of the State must be the first consideration," he wrote in the *Réflexions sur le Métier de Roi.* . . . When one has the State in view, one is working for oneself. The good of the one makes the glory of the other." The identity of the two interests was simply a matter of good sense in his opinion. " The prince alone should have the sovereign direction of affairs," he said in his

Memoirs ; " because he alone has no other fortune to establish but that of the State, no acquisition to make save for the aggrandisement of the monarchy, . . . no authority to invoke except that of the laws, no debts to pay except the public charges, and no friends to enrich except his people."

Another feature of the royal counsel is founded on his moderation and prudence. In many places Louis XIV recommends the Dauphin to keep himself well-informed, to take counsel, to work, to learn, and to distrust flatterers. He shows the usefulness of prudent action, and the need to avoid all precipitation : " It is far better to bring a matter to its achievement later on than to ruin it through precipitation."

He applied this policy of moderation to the Protestants by precepts which may, perhaps, seem astonishing coming from Louis XIV. He advocated the form of justification which, 450 years before, the great Pope Innocent III had deemed the most effective in regard to the Greeks, namely, the example of an edifying life on the part of the representatives of Catholicism. " I resolved," he wrote, " to rouse the Bishops, as far as in me lay, to work for their enlightenment and to remove from their body the scandals which sometimes separated them from us ; to place no one in these high places, nor in any other to which I have the power of nomination, except men of piety, application, and knowledge, men able to repair by altogether different conduct the disorders which that of their former predecessors had in large measure caused in the Church."

All through the Memoirs we discern natural political good sense which cannot fail to strike the reader. In this connection, Sainte-Beuve liked to compare the Great King with Saint-Simon who was harsh and

unjuſt towards his memory and who had, notwith-
ſtanding, *senti son maître en l'approchant.* " If (which
could never have happened) a conversation on politics
were to have taken place between the two," wrote Sainte-
Beuve, " Louis XIV would have preserved on essential
points his sovereign superiority in a simple tone, and
with his ready good sense. Let us leave to each the
name which properly describes him. Saint-Simon was a
great portrayer and a profound moraliſt ; Louis XIV
was a King."

This figure of a king ſtands out marvellously clear
in reading the Memoirs. " Greatness, order, and
beauty " were the things that intereſted Louis XIV in
the world, and his ideal is read in those words. The
man appears, too, throughout the work, the young hero
of 1666, who was to win the name of Grand Roi.

In reality, there was something of the heroic about
him after the manner of the princes of the Italian Renais-
sance. Young, self-assured, attractive, and triumphant,
he loved glory as a noble miſtress. " The ardour which
one feels for it," he wrote, " is not one of those feeble
passions which diminish with possession. Its favours,
which are never won save by effort, likewise never produce
diſtaſte, and whosoever can bring himself to desire no
fresh ones is unworthy of all those he has received."

Mazarin was a good judge when he said that he had
in him " enough ſtuff to make four kings and one upright
man." To a love of glory he added a natural majeſty,
and the proper sense of what was expeéted from a king,
as well as an aſtonishing faculty for applying himself
to what he called his *métier.* The *métier de roi,* he
says with grave enthusiasm, " is a great one, noble and
pleasing when one feels oneself to be worthy of acquitting
oneself well in all things undertaken." The greatness

which he shows did not proceed from personal vanity, but from his consciousness of the charge he had assumed : " If I can make my meaning clear to you," he says to his son, " it seems to me that we should be humble in regard to ourselves, and proud in regard to the position we occupy."

In upholding this position he was aided by his application to work and his faculty of assimilation. " Born," as Saint-Simon says, " with a mind able to mould, polish, and refine itself, and to learn from others without copying them, and without effort," he knew how to enrich his political sense by turning everything and every one to good account. The secret of his royal genius was the marvellous use he made of the experience of his counsellors and of the lessons to be learned from events, thanks to that remarkable good sense which formed the foundation of his character.

Good sense and good judgment, together with glory, formed his great passion. How many times these words recur in the Memoirs ! " The function of Kings," he wrote, " consists principally in allowing good sense to act, which always acts naturally and without effort." This sentence very well sums up the Memoirs and the King's way of thinking. As Sainte-Beuve says, " He makes us feel the charming quality there is in the exercise of good sense. He believed that good sense, when put to the test of practice and experience, is the best counsellor and the surest guide." The sound reason which directed his reflections dictated to him those precepts whose meticulous sagacity, prudence, and moderation very often astonish us in this sovereign of twenty-eight years, whom one is not accustomed to consider in this light. And sometimes it inspires in him fine moral observations which remind us that Louis XIV was contemporary

with those moralists who are the honour and distinguishing mark of French literature.

With his love of reason, his psychological realism,
and his early proficiency, Louis XIV as a writer was
closely related to the school of 1660—to Boileau, Racine,
and Molière, men of the same age, or a little older.
It is no abuse of the word " classic," which is again
coming into fashion, to say this of him ; he was classic
in politics, just as those poets and dramatists, and we
like to recall how he seconded their efforts. Sainte-
Beuve, to whom we must continually refer, has already
noted the affinity existing between the King's work
and that of the great classics. Having in mind the King's
advice to avoid all hurry, he wrote : " I find a wonderful
agreement in the point of view and the action of Louis
XIV with that of the distinguished men of his time.
Boileau counselled a man to go over his work twenty
times, and taught Racine to write at great pains his
easy flowing lines. Louis gave to his son absolutely
similar and analogous precepts in connection with
politics ; he counselled him to go over any plan in his
mind twenty times before putting it into execution, and endeavoured to teach him to arrive at the
readiest solution of each matter with deliberation. In
the same way, in many a moral reflection with
which he intermingled politics, Louis XIV showed
himself to be a worthy contemporary of Nicole and
Bourdaloue."

Between the King and the great minds of his time
there existed a harmony which favoured the development
of this grand period. We need have no doubt that the
same spirit which directed the compilation of the Memoirs
assured the triumph of classic literature. Sainte-Beuve
gives us an insight into this when asking what would

have been the course of French literature but for the influence of the young King : " The literary tendencies in evidence on the morrow of the Fronde and anterior to Boileau and Racine, had they not been restrained by the eye of the King would have become further developed, and more and more emancipated under a Mæcenas who would have been far from severe. We can see that they were quite ready for this ; the spirit of libertinism and affectation were the sand-banks to be avoided ; fundamental corruption was showing itself. The young King came upon the scene, and brought with him and encouraged his youthful taste for literature ; he formed a corrective to the old, and, apart from some brilliant exceptions, impressed on the productions of his time, taken as a whole, the coherent and moral character which prevails in his own writings and in his own habit of mind."

The Memoirs of Louis XIV are thus closely allied to the great classic movement, and are an illustration of it. What a grand year was 1668 ! Racine produced the *Plaideurs* ; Molière *Amphitryon* and *l'Avare* ; Boileau wrote *l'Epître au Roi* ; La Fontaine published the first six books of his *Fables* ; and, in the leisure resulting from the peace which the glorious Treaty of Aix-la-Chapelle had just restored to France, Louis XIV began the compilation of his Memoirs.

The value of the royal work did not escape those who made use of it. It will be sufficient to mention three great minds living at different periods—Voltaire, Chateaubriand, and Sainte-Beuve. Voltaire, through the instrumentality of the Maréchal de Noailles, was acquainted with the fragment which has been called *Réflexions sur le Métier de Roi*. " This seems to me," he said to the Maréchal, " to be one of the finest monuments to his glory ; it is well conceived, well done, and shows an *esprit juste et une grande âme.*"

Chateaubriand knew the Memoirs in the edition of 1806, and gave expression to the happy discovery of the real man which this work affords : " The Memoirs of Louis XIV will increase his renown ; they disclose nothing base, they reveal none of those shameful secrets which the heart of man too often hides in the deep recesses of his soul. Seen at closer quarters, and in the private intimacy of his life, Louis XIV does not cease to be Louis le Grand ; one is charmed that such a *beau buste* did not have a *tête vide*, and that his inner soul corresponded to his noble exterior."

Let us listen once more to Sainte-Beuve, who, in one of his *Lundis*, brought out better than any one the merit of the royal work. He anticipates the criticisms which might be made, and have not failed to be made, of the self-praise which the King metes out to himself in explaining his political methods ; but, while making all due reservations, he thinks this affords a better way of forming a judgment, even of this favourable aspect of the great King : " He takes himself naturally as the type and figure of an accomplished prince ; he sees himself as already established and facing posterity. But it is more profitable to insist on the lofty incentives he found in this royal assurance and consciousness." If nothing but a panegyric of Louis XIV written by himself can be seen in the Memoirs, we may be sure we have not understood them at all, and have, in addition, misconceived the Prince's consciousness of his own *métier* when he wrote them in the interests of all—of the Dauphin, and of the kingdom.

It seems that Louis XIV did not give his Memoirs

to the Dauphin, for whom they had been written, until rather later on, between 1674 and 1677, when the latter came of royal age. Bossuet and Montausier had been attending to his moral and religious inftruction up till that time, and Louis then thought of completing his education with a political grounding.

If the Dauphin did not have an opportunity to put these lessons into practice, they were not loft ; through the Maréchal de Noailles they entered into the royal tradition. The same de Noailles who had rescued the papers of Louis XIV became the guide of Louis XV in his happy essays at personal government, when that sovereign, at laft rid of the tutelage of Fleury, determined, in 1743, to govern by himself, and aftounded France, overjoyed at having again found a King, to whom they gave the title of *Bien-Aimé*. The counsels lavished by de Noailles on him were those which Louis XIV had set forth in writing, and to give them greater weight he communicated to Louis XV the papers of the Great King.

Louis XVI also made use of the work. In 1786, he charged General Grimoard with the preparing of a work for the education of his children which he wished to direct himself. He put into his hands a copy of the Memoirs, bidding him classify the different portions and add explanations. It was this copy, remaining in the hands of Grimoard by force of subsequent circum-ftances, which occasioned the edition of 1806, the preparation of which the general entrufted to Grouvelle.

The work of Louis XIV as a matter of fact did not see the light of day until the year 1806, when two editions appeared simultaneously. Less fortunate than Sully's *Economies Royales*, or Richelieu's *Teftament Politique*, it had to wait nearly 150 years before becoming known in its entirety to the public. In 1671 Pellisson had revealed its exiſtence to the Académie, and in 1677 the associates had proposed as the subjeƈt of their competition the care taken by the King " de dresser lui-même les Mémoires de son règne pour servir d'inſtruƈtions " to the Dauphin. But subsequently it had fallen into semi-oblivion.

Voltaire recalled attention to the writings of the King in his *Siècle de Louis XIV*, in which he inserted the *Réflexions sur le Métier de Roi* and the *Inſtructions à Philippe V*. Then in 1767, some years after de Noailles had placed the manuscripts of Louis XIV in the Bibliotheque, the Abbé Olivet published fragments of the Memoirs, which were re-edited in 1789 by Sautreau de Marsy. In 1806, Gain-Montagnac and Grouvelle each brought out their edition based on different renderings. The beſt, that by Grouvelle, is not without its defeƈts ; in addition to reproducing for the years 1661 and 1662 the copy given by Louis XVI to Grimoard (the origin of which we are ignorant of, as well as its present fate), Grouvelle followed for the year 1666 the second rendering of the Memoirs and not, as he should have done, the third and laſt, which Dreyss reſtored.

In spite of its defeƈts, Grouvelle's edition has done a great service ; it has truly revealed the Memoirs of Louis XIV. Who can say whether the edition by Dreyss, scholarly and intereſting as it is to any one desirous of following ſtep by ſtep the King's work, has not after all done it a bad service, and, through rendering it difficult to read, has not been largely responsible for the faƈt that the Memoirs are so little known despite their celebrity ? Naturally desirous of emphasising Périgny's collaboration, a discovery made by himself, he appears to have kept his eye on that alone, a defeƈt which is common to many inveſtigators ; and inſtead of giving Pellisson's revision for the year 1661, which the King had authorised as his own since it was made under his direƈtion, he prefers the anterior rendering by Périgny for reasons of personal taſte. It is juſt as if an editor of Balzac or Stendhal should go in search of a firſt manuscript and publish it in preference to the author-ised version as correƈted and acknowledged by the author.

. His wish, too, to present a critical edition led him to make all kinds of interpolations, juxtapositions, and references which render the reading of his two volumes a wearisome process. It is easy to see that he aƈted thus from his scruples as a hiſtorian, and with a view to giving authority for his ſtatements. But such a method is fallacious ; no one should run such a risk, and it is open to dispute whether it should be recognised. One is even tempted to say, although it would be a great injuſtice to the meritorious work by Dreyss, that a massacre of the text of Louis XIV has been the result which ſtrikes one moſt. Sainte-Beuve also did not hide this : " By submitting the reader to all the fatigue and labour which he himself had given to his inveſtigations and which he displays too complacently, the editor has rendered the reading of these Memoirs, agreeable as it is in the old and the *worse* edition, very difficult and troublesome in his own, which will henceforth pass for the only authentic and reliable one."

There is therefore room for a readable edition, and one which will conform to the wishes of Louis XIV ; that is to say, the authorised and laſt one to be revised and acknowledged by the King. This we have attempted as regards the two years in the Memoirs, the editing of which we have here undertaken. For the year 1661, we have adopted neither Grouvelle's nor Dreyss's text ; Dreyss preferred not to take Pellisson's text for his foundation, although Louis XIV had prepared, revised, corrected, and annotated it ; Grouvelle, it is true, gave Pellisson's text, but utilised a copy the origin of which he did not state, and whose present fate we do not know. Rather than follow only Grouvelle's edition which we have no means of correcting, we have had recourse to the manuscript written by Pellisson and revised by Louis XIV, the manuscript preserved in the Bibliothèque Nationale, where it was deposited by de Noailles in 1758. Moreover, this text differs very slightly from Grouvelle's.

For the year 1666, Grouvelle, using Périgny's revision for mere corrections, reproduced the second rendering written by a secretary. Dreyss has satisfactorily established that Périgny's text is really a third rendering, the last that we have, and consequently, in our opinion, the authorised text. We have therefore given this rendering as Dreyss did ; but by comparing the manuscripts we have been enabled in places to improve the text as published by him.

The spelling, which has no interest in itself for a work of this period, has been modernised. Proper names, as a rule, have been corrected, and we have introduced punctuation (as that of the manuscripts is rudimentary), while preserving as far as possible the breaks which occur.

We must now state the reasons which influenced our choice of the years 1661 and 1666. Both in matter and length they are the most important which were treated in either of the two portions of the Memoirs. The year 1661, which will give an idea of the work of Pellisson, presents a general view of the state of the kingdom at the commencement of personal government, and of the measures taken by Louis XIV to respond to this situation ; the year 1666, in which Périgny's collaboration is seen, shows us the King in full political, diplomatic, and military activity. These two years therefore offer the essence of the Memoirs, which we have less regret in dividing up because, inasmuch as they remained unfinished, they only constitute by themselves a fragmentary work.

To these portions of the Memoirs we have added three other writings by Louis XIV. The first is made up from notes written by the King in 1679, in view of a continuation of the Memoirs ; they are reflections on the necessity of inflicting punishment, in reference to the disgrace of Pomponne. This fragment—even if possibly it did not come from the actual hand of the King, it may very reasonably be supposed to have been dictated to a secretary—represents exactly the manner peculiar to Louis XIV, with its clear-cut and direct style, its concise, majestic, and charming eloquence, which admirably distinguish the Great King. Louis set store by these short reflections as forming an important part of his work, for we can find corrections in the shaky hand of the aged sovereign, which had of necessity been made at a much later date. They were published for the first time by Voltaire ; we have seen on a former page what the author of the *Siècle de Louis XIV* thought of them ; he justly adds that this writing " gives favourable testimony to posterity of the uprightness and magnanimity of his soul." In 1776, the Abbé Millot re-published it in his *Mémoires Politiques et Littéraires*, calling it *Réflexions sur le Métier de Roi et l'Administration des Affaires Etrangères*. The first portion of this title, slightly inaccurate perhaps, but more expressive, has since remained.

The two writings are in the King's own hand. Well worthy of being published for their own merits, these autograph texts will be interesting by the side of the Memoirs. In the *Instructions au Duc d'Anjou*, dated 1700, we shall again find that spirit of reason and those moral observations which characterise the work of the King thirty years before. In the *Projet de Harangue*, probably written in 1710, in the midst of the reverses of the War of the Spanish Succession, we cannot fail to notice an innate nobility and majesty, already very marked in the Memoirs, more noticeable still in the direct language which characterises pieces like the *Réflexions sur le Métier de Roi*, and rendered even still grander in this last owing to the tragic circumstances under which Louis XIV wrote it.

BIBLIOGRAPHICAL NOTE

THE MANUSCRIPTS OF THE TEXTS we are publishing are all in the Bibliothèque Nationale, where they were placed by the Maréchal de Noailles successively in 1749 and in 1758, when he entrusted to their keeping Pellisson's revision of the year 1661 by itself. The year 1661 takes up the whole of manuscript Fr. 10332 (ex 2282). The *cahiers* of the year 1666 are scattered through two volumes : Fr. 6733 (ex 2281, Vol II), folios 188 to 250 for *cahiers* 1 to 8, and folios 275 to 278 for *cahier* II ; Fr. 6734 (ex 2281, Vol. III), folios 189 to 205 for *cahiers* 9 and 10. Manuscript Fr. 10331 (ex 2280, Vol. III) contains the three other writings : the *Réflexions sur le Métier de Roi* in folios 125 to 130 ; the *Instructions au Duc d'Anjou* in folios 115 to 119 ; and the *Projet de Harangue* in folios 135 to 137.

The chief editions are : Grouvelle's *Œuvres de Louis XIV*, Paris, 1806, 6 vols ; and especially Dreyss's edition, *Mémoires de Louis XIV pour l'instruction du Dauphin*, Paris, 1860, 2 vols. Voltaire was the first to publish the *Réflexions sur le Métier de Roi* and a portion of the *Instructions au Duc d'Anjou*, in his *Siècle de Louis XIV* (2nd and following editions, chap. xxviii).

The most important of the critical studies and works bearing on the Memoirs, apart from the notices given by Grouvelle and Dreyss, are : Sainte-Beuve's study, dated 1852, in Vol. V of his *Lundis* ; Chéruel's study in the *Comptes-rendus de l'Académie des Sciences Morales et Politiques* for 1886, pp. 785-807 ; the article by Monsieur E. Bourgeois in the *Sources de l'Histoire de France, XVII Siècle*, Paris, 1913, Vol. II, p. 134 ; the *Œuvres de Colbert*, Clément's edition, Vol. II, pp. ccxii–ccxvii, and Vol. VI, pp. 464–490 ; and lastly, the introduction by Monsieur Jean de Boislisle to the *Mémoriaux du Conseil de* 1661, Paris, Société de l'Histoire de France, 1905, Vol. I.

MEMOIRS FOR THE YEARS
1661 AND 1666

BOOK I

1661

1661

MANY REASONS, all very important, my son, have decided me, at some labour to myself, but one which I regard as forming one of my greateſt concerns, to leave you these Memoirs of my reign and of my principal aƈtions. I have never considered that kings, feeling in themselves, as they do, all paternal affeƈtion, are dispensed from the obligation common to fathers of inſtruƈting their children by example and by precept. On the contrary, it has seemed to me that in the high rank in which we are placed, you and I, a public duty is added to private, and that in the midſt of all the respeƈt which is given us, all the abundance and brilliancy with which we are surrounded— which are nothing more than the reward accorded by Heaven itself in return for the care of the peoples and States confided to our charge—this solicitude would not be very lofty if it did not extend beyond ourselves by making us communicate all our enlightenment to the one who is to reign after us.

I have even hoped that in this purpose I might be able to be more helpful to you, and consequently to my subjects, than any one else in the world ; for there cannot be men who have reigned of more talents and greater experience than I, nor who have reigned in France ; and I do not fear to tell you that the higher the position the greater are the number of things which cannot be viewed or underſtood save by one who is occupying that position.

I have considered, too, what I have so often experienced myself—the throng who will press round you, each for his own ends, the trouble you will have in finding disintereſted advice, and the entire confidence you will be able to feel in that of a father who has no other intereſt but your own, no ardent wish but for your greatness.

I have also sometimes flattered myself with this thought, that if the occupations, pleasures, and affairs of the world, as too often happens, one day take you away from the ſtudy of books and hiſtory—the only one, nevertheless, in which young princes can find a thousand truths unmingled with flattery—the reading of these Memoirs may supply in some sort the place of any other, and may retain their savour and diſtinction in your eyes, from the affection and respect which you will preserve for me.

I have given, therefore, some consideration to the condition of Kings—hard and rigorous in this respect— who owe, as it were, a public account of their actions to the whole world and to all succeeding centuries, and who, nevertheless, are unable to do so to all and sundry at the time without injury to their greateſt intereſts, and without divulging the secret reasons of their conduct. And, not doubting that the somewhat important and considerable affairs in which I have taken part, both within and without my kingdom, will one day exercise diversely the genius and passions of writers, I should not be sorry for you to possess in these Memoirs the means of setting hiſtory aright if it should err or not rightly interpret, through not having faithfully reported or well divined my plans and their motives. I will explain them to you without disguise, even where my good intentions have not been happily conceived, being persuaded that only a small mind and one usually at fault could expect never to make a mistake, and that those who have sufficient merit to succeed the more often, discover some magnanimity in recognising their faults.

I know not whether I should account as a fault of my own not to have assumed at the beginning the conduct of my realm. If it be a fault, I have striven earnestly to repair it afterwards, and I make bold to assure you that this was never the result either of negligence or of slackness.

From my early infancy the very name of *rois fainéants* or *maires du palais* displeased me when mentioned in my presence.[1] But I must point out the state of affairs : grievous disturbances throughout the kingdom before and after my majority ; a foreign war in which these troubles at home had lost to France thousands and thousands of advantages ; a Prince of my blood and of great name at the head of my enemies ; many Cabals in the State ; the Parliaments still in the possession and enjoyment of a usurped authority ; at my Court very little disinterested fidelity and, on this account, my subjects, though outwardly most submissive, as much a responsibility and cause of misgiving to me as the most rebellious ; a minister re-established in power despite so many factions, very skilful and very adroit, but whose views and methods were naturally very different from mine, whom, nevertheless, I could not gainsay, nor abate the least portion of his credit, without running the risk of again raising against him by some misleading appearance of disgrace those very storms which had been allayed with so much difficulty. I myself was still very young, though I had reached the majority of kings, which the State laws anticipate in order to avoid still greater evils, but not the age at which mere private persons begin to regulate freely their own affairs. I only knew to its full extent the greatness of my burden, without having yet learned my own capabilities. Before all things, even before life itself, I placed firmly in my heart a lofty reputation, if so be I might acquire it, but I understood at the same time that my first moves would either lay its foundations or cause me to destroy all hopes of it for ever ; and thus I felt myself almost equally being urged on and held back in my aims by the one and only desire for renown.

I did not, however, neglect to prove myself in secret and without a confidant, reasoning alone and in my heart over all events as they occurred, full of hope and joy when I discovered sometimes that my first views became those which men of skill and experience arrived at in the end ; and I held firmly from the bottom of my heart that I should never have been placed and preserved on the throne animated by so great a passion to acquit myself well without being able to find the means to do so. Some years therefore having thus rolled by, the state of general peace, my marriage, my authority more firmly established, and the death of Cardinal Mazarin ² constrained me to defer no longer the putting into execution of the hopes and fears which I had entertained for so long.

I made a beginning by casting my eyes over all the different parties in the State,³ not indifferently, but with the glance of experience, sensibly touched at seeing nothing which did not invite and urge me to take it in hand, but carefully watching what the occasion and the state of affairs would permit. Everywhere was disorder. My Court as a whole was still very far removed from the sentiments in which I trust you will find it. Men of quality and officials, accustomed to continual intrigue with a minister who showed no aversion to it, and to whom it had been necessary, arrogated to themselves an imaginary right to everything that suited them. There was no governor of a city who was not difficult to govern ; no request was preferred without some complaint of the past, or some hint of discontent for the future, which I was allowed to expect and to fear. The favours demanded, and extorted, rather than awaited, by this one and that, and always considerable, no longer were binding on any one, and were only regarded as useful in order to maltreat thenceforth those to whom they wished me to refuse them.

The finances, which give movement and action to the great organisation of the monarchy, were entirely exhausted, so much so that we could hardly find the ways and means. Much of the most necessary and most privileged expenses of my house and of my own privy purse were in arrears beyond all that was fitting, or maintained only on credit, to be a further subsequent burden. At the same time a prodigality showed itself among public men, masking on the one hand their malversations by every kind of artifice, and revealing them on the other in insolent and daring luxury, as though they feared I might take no notice of them.

The Church, apart from its usual troubles, after lengthy disputes on matters of the schools, a knowledge of which they allowed was unnecessary to salvation for any one, with points of disagreement augmenting day by day through the heat and obstinacy of their minds, and ceaselessly involving fresh human interests, was finally threatened with open schism by men who were all the more dangerous because they were capable of being very serviceable and greatly deserving, had they themselves been less opinionated.4 It was not a question only of a few private and obscure professors, but of Bishops established in their Sees and able to draw away the multitude after them, men of high repute, and of piety worthy of being held in reverence had it been accompanied by submission to the sentiments of the Church, by gentleness, moderation, and charity. Cardinal de Retz, Archbishop of Paris, whom for well-known reasons of State I could not permit to remain in the kingdom, encouraged all this rising sect from inclination or interest, and was held in favour by them.5

The least of the ills affecting the order of Nobility was the fact of its being shared by an infinite number of usurpers possessing no right to it, or one acquired by money without any claim from service rendered. The tyranny exercised by the nobles over their vassals and neighbours in some of my provinces could no longer be suffered or suppressed save by making severe and rigorous examples. The rage for duelling—somewhat modified by the exact observance of the latest regulations, over which I was always inflexible—was only noticeable in a now well advanced recovery from so inveterate an ill, so that there was no reason to despair of the remedy.

The administration of Justice itself, whose duty it is to reform others, appeared to me the most difficult to reform. An infinity of things contributed to this state of affairs : the appointments filled haphazard or by money rather than by selection and merit ; scant experience and less knowledge on the part of some of the judges ; the regulations referring to age and service almost every-where eluded ; chicanery firmly established through many centuries, and fertile in inventing means of evading the most salutary laws. And what especially conduced to this was the fact that these insatiable gentry loved litigation and fostered it as their own peculiar property, applying themselves only to prolong and to add to it.[6] Even my Council, instead of supervising the other jurisdictions, too often only introduced disorder by issuing a strange number of contrary regulations, all in my name and as though by my command, which rendered the confusion far more disgraceful.

All this collection of evils, their consequences and effects, fell principally upon the people, who, in addition, were loaded with impositions, some crushed down by poverty, others suffering want from their own laziness since the peace, and needing above all to be alleviated and occupied.

Amid so many difficulties, some of which appeared to be insurmountable, three considerations gave me courage. The first was that in these matters it is not in the power of Kings—inasmuch as they are men and have to deal with men—to reach all the perfection they set before themselves, which is too far removed from our feebleness ; but that this impossibility of attainment is a poor reason for not doing all we can, and this difficulty for not always making progress. This, moreover, is not without its uses, nor without glory. The second was that in all just and legitimate enterprises, time, the fact of doing them even, and the aid of Heaven, open out as a rule a thousand channels, and discover a thousand facilities which we had not looked for. And the last was one which of itself seemed to me to hold out visibly that help, by disposing everything to the same end with which it inspired me.

In fact, all was calm everywhere. There was no movement, nor fear or seeming of any movement in my kingdom which might interrupt or oppose my designs. Peace was established with my neighbours, and to all seeming for as long as I myself wished it, owing to the conditions of affairs then prevailing.

Spain was not in a position to recover very promptly from her grievous losses.7   Not only was she without resources, but even without credit, and incapable of any great effort either in money or men, and occupied with her war with Portugal, which it would have been easy for me to render more difficult, and which the majority of the Grandees of the kingdom were suspected of not wishing to be finished.   The King was old and in doubtful health ; he had only one son of tender years who was also rather delicate ; he and his minister, Don Louis de Haro, were both fully informed on all the further consequences that war might bring, and it was not to their interest either from the state of the nation or of the Royal House.

I did not see anything to be feared from the Emperor,8 who had been chosen solely because he belonged to the House of Austria, and was tied in a thousand ways by an understanding with the States of the Empire ; he was somewhat inclined to undertake nothing on his own initiative, and his resolutions would follow his own mentality, rather than experience and dignity.9

The Electors who had in large measure imposed these hard conditions upon him and could be scarcely doubtful of his resentment, lived in continual distrust of him. Some of the other Princes of the Empire were working for my interests.10

Sweden could have genuine and lasting relations with me alone.   She had just lost a great Prince, and it was enough for her to safeguard her conquests during the infancy of her new King.11

Denmark, weakened by a previous war with her (Sweden), in which she had been near to complete exhaustion, only thought of peace and recuperation.12

England had hardly begun to breathe again after her

paſt troubles, and thought only of ſtrengthening her government under a newly reſtored King, who, besides, was favourably disposed towards France.¹³

The entire policy of the Dutch and their rulers had at that time only two ends in view : to foſter their commerce, and to humble the House of Orange. The leaſt little war would prejudice both, and their principal support lay in my friendship.¹⁴

Only the Pope in Italy,¹⁵ from what remained of his former hoſtility to Cardinal Mazarin, kept up a certain amount of ill feeling towards France, but it did no more than render difficult for me anything that might depend upon him, which in reality was nothing very considerable. His neighbours would not have followed his designs if he had made any againſt me. Savoy, which was governed by my Aunt,¹⁶ was very favourably disposed to me. Engaged in the war againſt the Turk, Venice sedulously maintained alliance with me, and looked for more from my support than from that of the other Chriſtian Princes.¹⁷ The Grand Duke¹⁸ renewed his alliance with me through the marriage of his son with a Princess of my blood. In a word, these Potentates, and all the others in Italy, of whom some were my friends and allies, such as Parma, Modena, and Mantua, were too feeble by themselves to injure me, and neither fear nor hope of advantage conſtrained them to league againſt me. I was even able to profit by what seemed to be a disadvantage ; no one in the great world yet knew me, but I was also less envied than I have been since ; my conduct was observed in a lesser degree, and others did not think so much of countering my designs.

It would assuredly have been to make a bad use of conditions of such perfect tranquillity, such as might only be met with very rarely in several centuries, not to turn them to the only account capable of making me appreciate them, at a time when my youth and the pleasure of being at the head of my armies would have caused me to wish to have more matters to deal with abroad. But inasmuch as my chief hope in these reforms was based on my will, their foundation at the outstart rested on making absolute my will by conduct which should impose submission and respect : by rendering scrupulous justice to all to whom I owed it ; but in the bestowing of favours, giving them freely and without constraint to whomsoever I would, and when it should please me, provided that my subsequent action should let others know that while giving reasons to no one for my conduct I ruled myself none the less by reason, and that in my view the remembrance of services rendered, the favouring and promoting of merit—in a word, doing the right thing—should not only be the greatest concern but the greatest pleasure of a prince.

Two things without doubt were absolutely necessary : very hard work on my part, and a wise choice of persons capable of seconding it.

As for work, it may be, my son, that you will begin to read these Memoirs at an age when one is far more in the habit of dreading than loving it, only too happy to have escaped subjection to tutors and to have your hours regulated no longer, nor lengthy and prescribed study laid down for you.

On this heading I will not warn you solely that it is none the less toil *by which* one reigns, and *for which* one reigns, and that the conditions of royalty, which may seem to you sometimes hard and vexatious in so lofty a position, would appear pleasant and easy if there was any doubt of your reaching it.

There is something more, my son, and I hope that your own experience will never teach it to you : nothing could be more laborious to you than a great amount of idleness if you were to have the misfortune to fall into it through beginning by being disgusted with public affairs, then with pleasure, then with idleness itself, seeking everywhere fruitlessly for what can never be found, that is to say, the sweetness of repose and leisure without having the preceding fatigue and occupation.

I laid a rule on myself to work regularly twice every day, and for two or three hours each time with different persons, without counting the hours which I passed privately and alone, nor the time which I was able to give on particular occasions to any special affairs that might arise. There was no moment when I did not permit people to talk to me about them, provided that they were urgent ; with the exception of foreign ministers who sometimes find too favourable moments in the familiarity allowed to them, either to obtain or to discover something, and whom one should not hear without being previously prepared.[19]

I cannot tell you what fruit I gathered immediately I had taken this resolution. I felt myself, as it were, uplifted in thought and courage ; I found myself quite another man, and with joy reproached myself for having been too long unaware of it. This first timidity, which a little self-judgment always produces and which at the beginning gave me pain, especially on occasions when I had to speak in public, disappeared in less than no time. The only thing I felt then was that I was King, and born to be one. I experienced next a delicious feeling, hard to express, and which you will not know yourself except by tasting it as I have done. For you must not imagine, my son, that the affairs of State are like some

49

obscure and thorny path of learning which may possibly have already wearied you, wherein the mind ſtrives to raise itself with effort above its purview, more often to arrive at no conclusion, and whose utility or apparent utility is repugnant to us as much as its difficulty. The funₑtion of Kings consiſts principally in allowing good sense to act, which always aₑts naturally and without effort. What we apply ourselves to is sometimes less difficult than what we do only for our amusement. Its usefulness always follows. A King, however skilful and enlightened be his miniſters, cannot put his own hand to the work without its effeₑt being seen. Success, which is agreeable in everything, even in the smalleſt matters, gratifies us in these as well as in the greateſt, and there is no satisfaₑtion to equal that of noting every day some progress in glorious and lofty enterprises, and in the happiness of the people which has been planned and thought out by oneself. All that is moſt necessary to this work is at the same time agreeable ; for, in a word, my son, it is to have one's eyes open to the whole earth ; to learn each hour the news concerning every province and every nation, the secrets of every court, the mood and the weaknesses of each Prince and of every foreign miniſter ; to be well-informed on an infinite number of matters about which we are supposed to know nothing ; to elicit from our subjeₑts what they hide from us with the greateſt care ; to discover the moſt remote opinions of our own courtiers and the moſt hidden intereſts of those who come to us with quite contrary professions. I do not know of any other pleasure we would not renounce for that, even if curiosity alone gave us the opportunity.

I have dwelt on this important subjeₑt longer than I had intended, and far more for your sake than for my own ; for while I am disclosing to you these methods and these alleviations attending the greatest cares of royalty I am not unaware that I am likewise depreciating almost the sole merit which I can hope for in the eyes of the world. But in this matter, my son, your honour is dearer to me than my own ; and if it should happen that God call you to govern before you have yet taken to this spirit of application and to public affairs of which I am speaking, the least deference you can pay to the advice of a father, to whom I make bold to say you owe much in every kind of way, is to begin to do and to continue to do for some time, even under constraint and dislike, for love of me who beg it of you, what you will do all your life from love of yourself, if once you have made a beginning.

I gave orders to the four Secretaries of State no longer to sign anything whatsoever without speaking to me ; likewise to the Controller, and that he should authorise nothing as regards finance without its being registered in a book which must remain with me, and being noted down in a very abridged abstract form in which at any moment, and at a glance, I could see the state of the funds, and past and future expenditure.

The Chancellor received a like order, that is to say, to sign nothing with the seal except by my command, with the exception only of letters of justice, so called because it would be an injustice to refuse them, a procedure required more as a matter of form than of principle; and I allowed to remain the administering and remissions of cases manifestly pardonable, although I have since changed my opinion on this subject, as I will tell you in its proper place. I let it be understood that whatever the nature of the matter might be, direct application must be made to me when it was not a question that depended only on my favour ; and to all my subjects without distinction I gave liberty to present their case to me at all hours, either verbally or by petitions.

At first petitions came in very great numbers, which nevertheless did not discourage me.[20] The disorder in which my affairs had been placed was productive of many ; the novelty and expectation, whether vain or unjust, attracted not less. A large number were presented connected with law-suits, which I could not and ought not to take out of the ordinary tribunals in order to have them adjudicated before me. But even in these things, apparently so unprofitable, I found great usefulness. By this means I informed myself in detail as to the state of my people ; they saw that I was mindful of them, and nothing won their heart so much. Oppression on the part of the ordinary tribunals might be represented to me in such a way as to make me feel it desirable to gain further information in order to take special measures when they were required. One or two examples of this kind prevented a thousand similar ills ; the complaints, even when they were false and unjust, hindered my officers from giving a hearing to those which were more genuine and reasonable.

Regarding the persons whose duty it was to second my labours, I resolved at all costs to have no prime minister ; and if you will believe me, my son, and all your successors after you, the name shall be banished for ever from France, for there is nothing more undignified than to see all the administration on one side, and on the other, the mere title of King.

To effect this, it was necessary to divide my confidence and the execution of my orders without giving it entirely to one single person, applying these different people to different spheres according to their diverse talents, which is perhaps the firſt and greateſt gift that Princes can possess.

I also made a resolution on a further matter. With a view the better to unite in myself alone all the authority of a maſter, although there muſt be in all affairs a certain amount of detail to which our occupations and also our dignity do not permit us to descend as a rule, I conceived the plan, after I should have made choice of my miniſters, of entering sometimes into matters with each one of them, and when they leaſt expeſted it, in order that they might underſtand that I could do the same upon other subjeſts and at any moment. Besides, a knowledge of some small detail acquired only occasionally, and for amusement rather than as a regular rule, is inſtruſtive little by little and without fatigue, on a thousand things which are not without their use in general resolutions, and which we ought to know and do ourselves were it possible that a single man could know and do everything.

It is not so easy for me to tell you, my son, what ought to be done in the choice of different miniſters. In this matter fortune plays always, in spite of us, as large or a greater part than sagacity ; and in the part that sagacity is able to play, intuition can do far more than taking thought.

Neither you nor I, my son, will seek out men for those kinds of employment whom diſtance or their own obscurity hides from our view, whatever be the capability they may possess. Of necessity, one muſt decide from a small number whom chance presents, that is to say, from among those who are already occupying some poſt, or men whose birth or inclination have placed neareſt to us.

And for this art of knowing men, which will be so important to you, not only in this matter, but in all the occasions of your life, I will tell you, my son, that it is one that may be learnt, but cannot be taught.

In reality, it is doubtless right to take largely into account a man's general and established reputation, because the public is not consulted in the appointment, and cannot easily be imposed upon for long. It is a wise thing to hear every one, and not to believe entirely those who approach us with regard to their enemies over and above the good which they are compelled to recognise in them, nor with regard to their friends over and above the evil which they endeavour to excuse in them ; it is still wiser to prove in small matters those whom one wishes to employ in greater. But the essence of the precepts for distinguishing clearly the talents, inclinations, and the tendency of each, is to make it a study and take pleasure in it ; and this I exhort you to do, for, as a rule, from the smallest to the greatest things, you will never understand one of them if you do not make it a pleasure and like doing it.

In this division of offices which I made, the persons I used the more often in matters of conscience were my confessor, Père Annat, whom I held in especial esteem for his upright and disinterested mind, and because he never mingled in any intrigue ; Marca, the Archbishop of Toulouse, whom I afterwards made Archbishop of Paris, a man of profound knowledge and very clear mind ; the Bishop of Rennes, because the Queen, my Mother, wished it, and the Bishop of Rodez, since Archbishop of Paris, who had been my tutor.[21]

In questions connected with the administration of justice, I communicated especially with the Chancellor, an officer of very long standing, and generally recognised as being very skilful in these matters.[22]

I called him also to all the public Councils which I

myself held, and particularly on two days of the week with the four Secretaries of State for the dispatch of ordinary affairs within the kingdom and for replies to petitions.

I also determined to be present sometimes at the different Adminiſtrative Councils held on my behalf, at which it was only a queſtion of regulating matters between the various jurisdictions. And if more important occupations spare you the time, you will do well to use it sometimes in this way in order by your presence to encourage in their duty those taking part, and to become personally acquainted with the Magiſtrates who report and give their opinion on the cases. From this assembly the men are chosen, as a rule, for governorships of provinces, for Embassies, and for other great poſts.

But as regards the moſt important intereſts of the State and secret matters wherein a small number of heads is to be desired as much as anything else, and which of themselves require more time and more application than all the reſt put together, in my wish not to confide them to one miniſter alone I considered Le Tellier, Fouquet, and Lionne to be the three possessing the beſt capacity to serve them usefully.[23]

The office of Secretary of State, which for twenty years had been exercised by Le Tellier with great devotion and assiduity, gave him a great knowledge of affairs.[24] He had been employed all that time on moſt confidential matters. Cardinal Mazarin had often told me that he had recognised his capability and fidelity on the moſt delicate occasions, as had I too myself. His conduct was sagacious, prudent, and modeſt, on which I set great ſtore.

Lionne had like teſtimony from Cardinal Mazarin, by whom he had been schooled.[25] I knew that not one of my subjects had been employed in foreign negotiations more often than he, or with greater success. He knew the different Courts of Europe, spoke and wrote fluently several languages, and had a taste for literature, and a ready, supple, and adroit mind suited to this kind of commerce with foreigners.

As for Fouquet,[26] people will think it strange that I wished to use him when they learn that his peculations were known to me at the time ; but I was aware that he had spirit and a great knowledge of internal affairs. And this made me conceive that, provided he acknowledged his past faults, he might render me good service.

However, to make sure of him I gave him Colbert, under the title of Intendant, as his controller in the finances, a man in whom I had every confidence because I knew that he was possessed of great application, intelligence, and probity, and I entrusted him from that time with the keeping of the register of the accounts of which I have spoken.[27]

I have learnt since that the choice of these three ministers had been diversely considered according to the different interests into which the world is divided. But, in order to know if I could have done better, it is only necessary to consider my other subjects to whom it was in my power to have given the same positions.

The Chancellor was in very truth a man of great skill, but more in matters of the administration of justice, as I have said, than in State affairs. I knew him to be very devoted to my service, but he was reputed not to possess all the firmness necessary in important matters. His age, and the continual occupations of such a laborious office, might render him less assiduous and less adapted to follow me to all those places to which the requirements of the realm and foreign wars might take me. Besides, his position was so great in itself in his quality of first officer in the kingdom, and President of all the Councils, that if it had been joined to a close participation in secret matters, it would have seemed, at any rate at that time, to render one of my ministers too great, and to raise him above the others, which I did not wish.

The Comte de Brienne, Secretary of State in the Foreign Department, was old, and presumed much on himself, and, as a rule, did not view matters either in my light or by reason.[28]

His son, who held the succession of his office, appeared to have the intention of doing well ; but he was so young that, far from taking his advice on my other interests, I could not even entrust him with the carrying out of his own work, which was in large measure performed by Lionne.

La Vrillière and du Plessis were good sort of people, but their lights were only proportioned to the discharge of their offices, in which nothing very important happened.[29]

I could, doubtless, have discovered men of higher consideration, but not of greater capacity than these three ; and a small number, as I have already said, appeared to me to be better than a larger.

To lay bare to you all that was in my mind, it was not to my interest to choose subjects of a more eminent quality. Before all else it was needful to establish my own reputation, and to let the public know from the very rank from which I chose them, that it was my intention not to share my authority with them. It was important that they should not conceive hopes of higher things than what it pleased me to give them—a matter which is difficult in the case of people of high birth. And these precautions were so necessary that even on that question the world was a fairly long time in getting to know me thoroughly.

Several were able to persuade themselves that within a short time some one of those who approached me would take possession of my mind and my affairs. The greater number regarded the assiduity of my labours as a fervour which would soon relax, and those willing to judge it more favourably were waiting to form their opinion by results.

Time has shown what to believe, and I have now been pursuing for ten years fairly consistently, as it seems to me, the same course, without relaxing my application ; kept well informed of everything ; listening to the least of my subjects ; at any hour knowing the number and quality of my troops, and the state of my fortified towns ; unremitting in issuing my orders for all their requirements ; dealing at once with foreign ministers ; receiving and reading dispatches ; doing myself a portion of the replies and giving to my secretaries the substance of the others ; regulating the State receipts and expenditure ; requiring those whom I placed in important posts to account directly to me ; keeping my affairs to myself as much as any one before me had ever done ; distributing my favours as I myself chose, and retaining, if I mistake not, those who served me in a modest position which was far removed from the elevation and power of prime ministers, although loading them with benefits for themselves and their belongings.

The observation by others of all these things doubtless gave rise to some opinion of me in the world ; and this opinion has in no small measure contributed to the success of what I have since undertaken, inasmuch as nothing could have produced such great results in so short a time as the reputation of the Prince.

But do not be deceived, my son, as so many others, and do not think that it will be time enough to establish it when the need for it arises. One does not realise it by means of armies ; it is useless to open one's treasures to acquire it. It must be looked to beforehand, and it is also only very long possession which makes it sure.

From the first years I had, to all outside appearances, good reason to be satisfied with my conduct ; but the praise which this novelty drew upon me did not fail to cause perpetual uneasiness in me, from the fear I then had, and from which even now I am not wholly exempt, of not having sufficiently merited it.

Any one will tell you how distrustful I was of my courtiers on that account, and how often with the view of testing their dispositions, I drew them on to praise the very things in which I thought I had failed, in order to reproach them at once, and accustom them not to flatter me.

But however veiled their intentions may have been, I will teach you, my son, a method by which it is easy to profit from all that they may say in praise of you, and that is to examine yourself secretly, and to trust to your own heart more than to their flattery ; estimate it always according to the mood of those who shall give expression to it, either for a spiteful reproach for some mistake committed against their interests, or a covert exhortation to some course foreign to your purpose ; persuaded, further, that you have not done enough, even when you may think you have deserved it ; and that a reputation cannot be sustained without every day acquiring a greater; and lastly, that glory is a mistress whom one is never able to neglect, and of whose first favours one cannot prove worthy if one does not ceaselessly desire fresh ones.

BOOK II

FIRST SECTION

THE GENERAL DISPOSITIONS on which I have been speaking occupied me all the month of March, for Cardinal Mazarin had only died on the 9th. And although in the course of his illness, which was of long duration, and for some time before, I had been observing with more than usual care the ſtate of affairs, I did not feel I ought to mingle in their detail until after an account had been given to me severally by all those who had shared with him in their adminiſtration, and ascertaining carefully the views they had held up till then or might entertain for the future, persuaded that my knowledge, even though it might be greater, could be greatly assiſted and greatly added to by theirs.

It has seemed necessary to me to impress upon you, my son, from fear of an excess of good intentions in your firſt youth, and from the very ardour which these Memoirs may arouse in you, that you should not confound two very different things : I mean the ruling of oneself, and the giving heed to no advice, which latter might be as dangerous an extreme as that of being ruled by others. The clevereſt private individuals take advice from other clever people about their little concerns. What should be the rule for Kings who have in their hands the public weal, and whose resolutions harm or benefit the whole earth ? Decisions of such importance should never be formed, if possible, without calling upon all the moſt enlightened, reasonable and wise among our subjeċts.

Necessity reduces us to a small number of persons chosen from the reſt, and whom it would not be politic to negleċt. You will find out, moreover, my son, what I soon recognised, that by talking over our affairs when no other personal consideration should stand in our way, we learn not only much about others, but also about ourselves. The mind brings to fruition its own thoughts by giving them the light of day, whereas, before, it held them in confusion, undeveloped, and rough-hewn. Discussion, which excites and warms it, carries it insensibly from objeċt to objeċt further than solitary and silent meditation had done, and opens out a thousand fresh expedients from the very difficulties opposed to it.

Besides, our lofty position in some way separates us from our people to whom our miniſters are closer, and are consequently able to see a thousand things of which we know nothing, but on which nevertheless we must make up our minds and take measures. Add to this their age, experience, deliberations, and their greater liberty to obtain information and suggeſtions from their inferiors, who in their turn gather them from others, ſtep by ſtep down to the loweſt.

But when, on important occasions, they have reported to us all the aspeċts and all the opposing reasons, all that is done elsewhere in similar cases, all that has been done formerly, and all that might be done to-day, it is incumbent upon us, my son, to choose what muſt be aċtually done. And in regard to that choice I will make bold to tell you that if we do not lack good sense or courage there is no other who can make a better one than us ; for to decide requires the *esprit de maître*, and without any comparison it is easier to do what one *is* than to imitate what one *is not*. And if we nearly always notice some difference between the private letters which we ourselves take the trouble to write, and those which our most skilled secretaries write for us, discovering in the latter a something less natural and the anxiety of a pen everlastingly in fear of saying too much or too little, have no doubt that in matters of the greatest consequence the difference will be still greater between our own resolutions and those which we leave our ministers to take without us ; wherein, the cleverer they are the more will they hesitate from fear of the issue, and owing to their responsibility will sometimes become embarrassed for quite a long time over difficulties which would not have delayed us for a moment.

Wisdom directs that on certain occasions we allow much to chance. In such cases reason herself counsels us to follow some kind of blind motion or instinct above itself which seems to come from Heaven and is known to all men, but is undoubtedly of greater weight and more worthy of consideration in the case of those whom it has itself placed in the first rank. No one can say when we should distrust or obey this motion ; neither books, nor rules, nor experience tell us ; a certain appropriateness, a certain daring of the mind, always more unfettered in a man who owes no account of his actions to any one, enables us to discover this.

However this may be, and not to allude again to the subject, immediately I had begun this system of conduct with my ministers I knew very well, not so much from what they said, but from a certain air of truth which detached itself from flattery, just as a living person differs from the most perfect statue (and it came back to me afterwards in many unsuspected ways), that they were not only satisfied but somewhat surprised to see me not accepting entirely all that they advised on the most difficult questions, and, while I did not affect to disregard it, taking my part so unconstrainedly, and following the line which more often than not subsequent events clearly showed to have been the better. And though they saw very well from that time onwards that they would always hold the proper position of ministers with me and nothing else, they were only the more pleased at the situation in which they were placed, with its thousand other advantages, of entire security for doing their duty in it. For there is nothing more dangerous to men occupying positions such as theirs as a King who is usually asleep, and wakes up with a start from time to time after losing the thread of affairs, and one who, in this uncertain and confused light, blames everybody for their want of success, for chance mishaps, or for faults for which he should accuse himself.

After having thus fully informed myself in private discussions with them I entered more boldly into practical action. There was nothing that appeared more pressing to me than to alleviate the condition of my people, to which the poverty of the provinces and the compassion I felt for them strongly urged me. The state of my finances, as I have shown you, seemed to oppose this, and in any case counselled delay ; but we must always be in haste to do well. The reforms I took in hand, though beneficial to the public, were bound to be irksome to a large number of private people. It was appropriate to make a beginning with something that could only be agreeable, and besides, there was no other way of maintaining any longer even the name of peace without its being followed by some sort of sop of this kind as a promise of greater hopes for the future. I therefore put aside any other considerations and, as a pledge of further alleviation, I first remitted three millions of the taxes for the following year which had already been prescribed and were awaiting collection.

At the same time, but with the intention of having them better observed than heretofore, I renewed the regulations against wearing gold and silver on clothes, and a thousand other foreign superfluities which were a kind of charge and contribution, outwardly voluntary but really obligatory, which my subjects, especially those most qualified and the persons at my Court, paid daily to neighbouring nations, or, to be more correct, to luxury and vanity.

For a thousand reasons, and also to pave the way for the reform of the administration of justice so greatly needed, it was necessary to diminish the authority of the chief jurisdictions which, under the pretext that their judgments were without appeal, and, as we say, sovereign and of final resort, regarded themselves as separate and independent sovereignties. I let it be known that I would no longer tolerate their assumptions. The *Cour des Aides* 30 in Paris having been the first to exceed its duties and in some degree its jurisdiction, I exiled a few of its most offending officers, believing that if this remedy were thoroughly employed at the outset, it would relieve me of the necessity of its frequent application afterwards ; and my action has been successful.

Immediately afterwards I gave them to understand my intentions still better in a solemn decree by my Supreme Council. For it is quite true that these jurisdictions have no cause to regulate each other in their different capacities, which are defined by laws and edicts. In former times these sufficed to make them live in peace

with each other, or in the event of certain differences
arising between them, especially in matters regarding
private individuals, these were so rare and so little
difficult of adjustment, that the Kings themselves decided
them with a word, more often than not during a walk,
on the report of the Magistrates, who then consisted
of a very small number, until, owing to the growth in
the kingdom of these matters and still more of chicanery,
this duty was entrusted principally to the Chancellor
of France and to the Administrative Council of which
I have spoken already to you. Now these officials of
necessity should be fully authorised to regulate the
competence of the other jurisdictions (and also all other
matters of which from time to time we deem it suitable
for reasons of public utility or of our own proper service,
to give them cognisance exceptionally) by taking it over
from them inasmuch as they derive their power only
from us. Notwithstanding, owing to this spirit of self-
sufficiency and the disorder of the times, they only yielded
in so far as seemed good to them, and outstepped their
powers daily and in all manner of cases in spite of their
proper limitations, often enough going so far as to say
that they recognised the King's will in no other form
than that contained in the Ordinances and the authorised
Edicts.

By this decree I forbade them all in general to give
any judgments contrary to those of my Council under
any pretext whatsoever, whether in their own jurisdiction
or in their private capacity, and I commanded them,
when one or the other felt they had suffered hurt to
make their complaint to me and have recourse to my
authority, inasmuch as I had only entrusted to them to
exercise justice towards my subjects and not to create
their own justice of themselves, which thing constitutes

a part of sovereignty so closely united to the Crown and so much the prerogative of the King alone that it cannot be communicated to any other.

In the same year, but a little later, for I shall not observe too closely the order of dates, in a certain matter connected with the finances of all the record offices in general, and one which they had never dared carry through in connection with those of the Parliament in Paris, because the property belonged to the officers of that body and sometimes to the chambers as a whole, I made it be seen that these officers must submit to the common law, and that there was nothing to prevent my absolving them from it when it pleased me to give this reward for their services.

About the same time, I did a thing which seemed even too bold, so greatly had the gentlemen of the law profited by it up till then, and so full were their minds of the importance they had acquired in the recent troubles through the abuse of their power. From three quarters I reduced to two all the fresh mortgages which were charged upon my revenue, which had been effected at a very extortionate rate during the war, and which were eating up the best of my farms of which the officials of the corporations had acquired the greater part. And this made them regard it as a fine thing to treat them as harshly as possible in their most vital interests. But at bottom this action of mine was perfectly just, for two quarters was still a great deal in return for what they had advanced. The reform was necessary. My affairs were not in such a state that I had nothing to fear from their resentment. It was more to the purpose to show them that I feared nothing they could do and that the times were changed. And those who from different interests had wished that these corporations might win the day learnt on the contrary from their submission what was due to me.

In all these matters, my son, and in several others which you will see afterwards, which have doubtless mortified my officers of juſtice, I do not wish you to attribute to me (as might those who know me less) motives of harshness, hatred, or vengeance on account of all that happened in the Fronde, in which one cannot deny that these corporations often forgot themselves even to ſtrange limits.

Their resentment, which at firſt appeared to be so juſt, may become less so if examined more closely. The jurisdiČtions have settled down of themselves and without trouble to their duties. The good servants have brought back the bad to better ways. Why impute to the whole body the faults of only a part, rather than the good service which has won the day? We should rather forget the one in favour of the other, and remember that, only to re-read hiſtory, there has hardly been any order in the Kingdom, Church, Nobility, Third Eſtate, which has not at some time blundered terribly and made amends.

Over and above this, my son, although in the matter of transgressions Kings are men as much or even more so than they are in other things, I do not fear to tell you that this is not so much the case when they are Kings in very truth, because an overmaſtering and dominating passion, that of their intereſts, their greatness, and their glory, ſtifles every other in them.

The pleasure which people imagine to lie in vengeance is hardly meant for us. It only flatters those whose power is in doubt, and this is so true that even private individuals in whom there is something of uprightness have difficulty in exercising it upon an enemy altogether beaten down and one who can have no hope of ever raising himself again. In our case, my son, we are only very rarely in the condition of finding pleasure in taking revenge ; for we have it in our power to do all things without constraint, or rather we find ourselves, on the contrary, in certain delicate and difficult positions which will not allow us to make trial of our power.

In short, as we belong to our people, so our people belong to us, and I have not yet seen that a wise man takes vengeance to his own prejudice by losing what belongs to him, under pretext that he has been ill served by it, instead of taking care to be better served for the future.

Therefore, my son, the resentment and anger felt by wise and skilful Kings against their subjects spring from nothing but justice and prudence.

The too great prominence of the Parliaments had been a danger to the whole kingdom during my minority. It was necessary to humble them, less for the evil they had already done than for what they might do in the future. Their authority, in so far as people regarded it as being in opposition to mine, produced very mischievous effects, however good their intentions may have been, and thwarted all my greatest and most useful measures. It was just that public utility should take the place of all other considerations, and reduce everything to their legitimate and natural order, even if (a thing which I have avoided nevertheless) it had been necessary to deprive this body of the power which had been given to it in former times ; just as the painter makes no difficulty in effacing with his own hand his most daring and beautiful work every time he finds it overdone and in plain disproportion with the rest of his work.

But I know, my son, and can sincerely protest to you,

that I had no aversion or rancour in my mind as regards my officers of juftice. On the contrary, if old age in men is venerable, it appeared ftill more so to me in this so ancient a body. I am persuaded that possibly in no other branch of my State is the work so great, nor the rewards smaller. I have for all of them the affe&ion and consideration that is their due ; and you, my son, who, according to all appearances will find them ftill further removed from these former vain pretensions, should pra&ise with all the more diligence what I myself do every day. I mean you should give them evidence on occasion of your efteem, you should know the chief representatives and those who possess the greateft merit, and let them see that you know them (for it is a gracious thing in a Prince to show that he is well informed on everything, and that duties performed far away from him are not loft) ; you should consider them and their families in the diftribution of appointments and emoluments, and favour their plans when they wish to attach themselves more particularly to you, and in a word, accuftom them to seeing you now and again by treating them well and giving them a friendly word inftead of encouraging the pra&ice of the paft century when it was one of their underftood rules not to go near the Louvre. And this was from no bad intention, but from the false idea of some imaginary opposition between the interefts of the Prince and those of the people whose defenders they conftituted themselves, not considering that these two interefts are only one, that the tranquillity of subje&s refts only on their obedience, that less harm results to the public by bearing with submission than by finding fault with even bad government by Kings, of whom God alone is the Judge, and that what they seem to be doing in opposition to the common law is more often based on reasons of State, which by universal consent form the firſt of all laws, but the leaſt underſtood and the moſt obscure to all who do not govern.

The smalleſt moves were important in these firſt beginnings which were showing France what was to be the charaĉter of my reign and of my conduĉt for the entire future. I was hurt by the way in which it had become cuſtomary to treat with the Prince, or rather with the miniſter, and I nearly always made it appear doubtful what they might expeĉt from my juſtice or benevolence.

The Convocation of the Clergy which had been sitting for a long time in Paris kept on putting off their departure, contrary to the expression of my wishes, until the issuing of certain decrees which they had demanded with insistence. I made them underſtand that they would gain nothing by these kind of devices. They broke up, and it was only then that the decrees were issued.

About this time the death of the Duc d'Epernon rendered vacant the appointment of Colonel-General of the French Infantry. His father, the firſt Duc d'Epernon, who had been elevated by the favour of Henri III, had lifted this office to the height of his ambition ; its power was infinite ; the nomination of subordinate officers attached to it gave power to the holder to place his creatures everywhere, and made him maſter of the principal forces of the State more than the King himself. I found it desirable to suppress this poſt, although I had previously curtailed in various ways these great powers in everything that decency and the times permitted.

As regards the governors of fortified places who so often abuse their powers, I firſt took away from them the financial subsidies which they had been allowed to levy during the war on the pretext of providing for the security of their cities without their having to wait for the money to be available, and of keeping them in good condition ; but as these contributions amounted to vaſt sums in the hands of private individuals, they rendered them too powerful and too absolute. Next, without being noticed, and little by little, I placed fresh troops in nearly all the garrisons, no longer suffering them to be composed of men dependent upon them as formerly, but, on the contrary, of many who knew only me. And what could not have been dared or thought of a few months previously was brought about easily and quietly, all looking to me, and in reality receiving more legitimate and juſter rewards for doing their duty.

I continued, however, the fortification of the château Trompette at Bordeaux, and the building of the citadel at Marseilles,[31] not so much that I had anything to fear in those two cities at the time, but to make sure of the future, and as an example to all the reſt. There was no unruly movement in the kingdom, but anything in the leaſt approaching disobedience, such as occurred occasionally at Montauban, at Dieppe, in Provence, and at Rochelle, was at once repressed and punished openly ; to effeċt which the peace, and the troops I had determined to maintain in good numbers, gave me sufficient means.

In a word, my son, I believed that, given the ſtate of things, a little severity was the greateſt kindness I could show to my people, a contrary disposition being bound to produce in them, of itself and in its consequences, an infinity of ills. For immediately a King slackens in what he has commanded, authority perishes, and with it all repose. Those who see a Prince at closer quarters, and are the firſt to learn his weakness, are also the firſt to abuse it ; after them come those in the second rank, and in the same way those in succession who hold some

sort of power. The full weight falls upon the lowest
ranks of the people, who by this means are oppressed by
thousands and thousands of petty tyrants, instead of
having a lawful King, whose indulgence nevertheless
has been the sole cause of all this disorder.

The marriage of my cousin of Orleans took place
about this time.³² I gave her a dowry from my own
funds and had her escorted at my expense to the States of
her father-in-law. But two other marriages of greater
importance deserve my mention to you.

That of my brother with the sister of the King of
England had been concluded in the month of March,³³
at which I had been greatly pleased, and for reasons of
State also ; for my alliance with that nation when under
Cromwell had, as it were, struck the last blow in the
Spanish wars, reducing my enemies to the position of
no longer being able to defend the Low Countries at
all, and consequently giving me also, had I wished, the
greatest advantages not accorded to me by the Treaty of
the Pyrénées. Matters in England had since changed
their aspect. Cromwell was dead, and the King re-
established on his throne. The Spaniards, getting
ready their resources for Flanders in case of a rupture
with me, and expecting nothing from Holland at the
time, were looking for any means to win over that Prince
to their interests. The marriage of my brother served
to retain him in my own ; but what I determined to
propose to the King himself on the part of the Princess of
Portugal, seemed as if it must take him away entirely
from Spain, and produce two other more considerable
results in my favour.³⁴ The first was to enable me to
uphold the Portuguese, whom I saw were in danger of
succumbing without my support ; the second was to
give me more freedom to aid them myself if I judged

this to be necessary, notwithstanding the Treaty of the Pyrénées which precluded me from doing so.[35]

I will here touch upon a question which is perhaps a more delicate one in the conduct of Princes than any other. I am very far from wishing to teach you infidelity, and I think I have shown to all Europe a short while back by the peace of Aix-la-Chapelle what great store I set on my word when once it has been given, preferring it exclusively to my greatest interests. But there is a distinction to be made in these matters which right judgment, equity, and conscience can make far better than any discourse. The position of the two Crowns of France and Spain is of such a kind to-day, and has long been so in the eyes of the world, that the one cannot be raised without lowering the other. This produces a jealousy between them which, if I may say so, is essential to them, also a kind of permanent hostility which treaties may hide but can never extinguish, because the root-cause always remains, and because either of them, working against the other, does not think so much of injuring the other as of maintaining and preserving himself—a duty which is so natural that it easily takes precedence of all others.

And to tell the truth, and without disguise, they never enter into any treaty but in this spirit. Whatever specious clauses referring to union and friendship are inserted with a view to procuring for themselves respectively all manner of advantages, the real sense understood very well by both from the experience of so many centuries is that each shall abstain from any kind of open hostilities and all demonstrations of bad faith ; for as regards secret infractions that will make no stir, each expects them from the other from the natural principle I have mentioned, and only promises the contrary in the same sense as the other has promised. And so we may say that each dispensing themselves in an equal degree from observing the treaties, there is no contravention strictly speaking, because the wording is not taken literally, although none other can be employed, just as is done in the world in the wording of compliments (to take a different kind of case) which are absolutely necessary in our daily intercourse, and are far less significant than they sound.

The Spaniards showed us the example first. Whatever the state of profound peace we were observing towards them, have they ever missed an occasion of fomenting disorders in our midst and our civil wars, and has their special quality as Catholics prevented them at any time from providing money surreptitiously to the rebel Huguenots ? They are constantly at pains to welcome with costly attentions all who leave this country in discontent, even nobodies and persons of no consideration ; not that they are ignorant of what condition they are, but to demonstrate by this means what they are ready to do for people of more importance. Lastly, I could not have any doubt that they had been the first to violate the Treaty of the Pyrénées,[36] and in a thousand different ways, and I should have felt myself to have been wanting in the duty I owe to my States if, through a more scrupulous observance than their own, I had allowed them a free hand to ruin Portugal in order to fall upon me afterwards with all their forces, and by troubling the peace of Europe to take back all that they had given me by that Treaty. As to the clauses in which they precluded me from rendering assistance to that still insecure Crown, the more unusual, oft-repeated and carefully safeguarded they were, the more did they make clear that they did not believe that I was bound to abstain from doing so ; and the only deference I thought I should observe towards these clauses consisted in only aiding them (the Portuguese) from necessity, secretly, with moderation and restraint. And this was possible in a more convenient manner through the interposition, and in the name of the King of England, when once he became the brother-in-law of the King of Portugal.

I overlooked nothing therefore in order to bring him to this alliance, and because his is a Court where as a rule much can be done by money, and the ministers of this nation generally have been very often suspected of being in the pay of Spain, and as the Chancellor Hyde,[37] a man very skilled in the interior affairs of the kingdom, at that time appeared to have great influence over the mind of the King, I entered into a very secret negotiation with him in particular, about which even my Ambassador in England knew nothing, and sent to him on different occasions a man of intelligence[38] who was known to him, and who, on the pretext of buying lead for my buildings, carried letters of credit to the amount of five hundred thousand pounds, which he offered to this minister on my part, without asking anything else but his friendship. He refused the offer, with all the more merit because at the same time he confessed to this envoy that he himself was in favour of the marriage with Portugal in the interests of the King, his master, to whom he afterwards spoke in secret about it.

The Spaniards, on their side, proposed the Princess of Parma, whom they offered to dower at their own expense as an Infanta ; then, when I had caused this proposition to be rejected, they brought forward the daughter of the Prince of Orange, offering the same advantages and showing themselves unmindful in this of their great zeal for the faith, and that to give to that State a Protestant Queen meant the taking away from the Catholics the sole consolation and the sole support which they might have hoped for on that question.

But I so contrived matters that this second proposition, like the first, was rejected, and even served to bring about more promptly what I wished for Portugal and their Infanta.

SECOND SECTION

T HIS WAS THE MOST IMPORTANT of all the foreign
affairs of this year. I will not omit alluding
here to some others of less consequence,
but which will make you see that while strengthening
as far as possible my authority within the kingdom
I did not forget to uphold the interests and the dignity
of the Crown, whenever it was called in question outside.

The Ambassadors of Genoa,39 by means of an oft-
repeated artifice, which they wished to render into a
kind of prerogative and right, for some years had been
usurping a claim to royal treatment at my Court. To
effect this they had subjected themselves to the practice
of never taking their audiences except on the same day
on which they were given to some King's Ambassador, in
order that by entering the Louvre immediately after him,
and to the same beating of the drums, it was impossible
to distinguish whether this honour had reference to them
or not. This vanity was all the more ridiculous because
this State, for long in the possession of our ancestors,
possesses no sovereignty except what it gave to itself
by its rebellion a hundred and forty or so years back,40
and belongs lawfully to us by several good titles such as
the solemn and voluntary treaties made by the whole
people with us, frequently renewed in full and entire
consent, and confirmed more than once by right of
arms. I gave these Ambassadors to understand how far

I was from suffering their mad pretensions which they had even dared to explain to me : Neither they nor their superiors have cared to speak about it since, trembling with fear on the contrary at the slightest movement of my troops in the direction of Italy, in the knowledge of what I might justly claim from them.

The Emperor had considered it to be in his interest to announce to me his election, as his predecessors had done to mine ; but he had conceived the fanciful idea that it was not consistent with his dignity to be the first to write to me, and had addressed his dispatch to the Spanish Ambassador, with orders not to deliver it into my hands until he had obtained from me some kind of complimentary letter which might make it seem that I had anticipated him. I not only refused to write him anything of the kind, but in order to teach that Prince the better to know me, I obliged him immediately afterwards to strike out from the apanages of his ministers the qualities of Comte de Ferrette and Landgrave of Alsace, these States having been ceded to me by the Treaty of Munster. I also made him withdraw from a projected league against the Turk the title of head of the Christian people, which he gave himself, as if he were really in possession of the same Empire and the same rights as had belonged to Charlemagne in former days after he had upheld the (Christian) religion against the Saxons, Huns, and Saracens.

And while on this subject, my son, for fear that people may sometimes wish to impose upon you by the fine names of Roman Empire, Cæsar, or the successors of those great Emperors from whom we ourselves derive our origin, I feel obliged to remark how far removed are the Emperors of to-day from that greatness whose titles they affect. When these titles were borne by our

House it reigned at one and the same time over France, the Low Countries, Germany, Italy, and the greater part of Spain which it had divided among divers individual seigneurs, reserving the suzerainty to itself. The sanguinary victories over several races who had come from the North and the South in order to overthrow Christianity had carried terror of the French name over all the earth. Charlemagne finally seeing no King in all Europe, nor, to speak truly, in all the world, to match himself, this name seemed to be inappropriate henceforth either for them or him from the inequality of their relative positions. He had already mounted to this lofty point of glory, not by the election of a few Princes, but by courage and victories which are the election and suffrages of Heaven itself, when he resolved to submit the other powers under one alone. No such extended dominion as his has ever been seen apart from the four famous monarchies to whom is commonly attributed the Empire over the whole world, although they never conquered or possessed any but a small portion of it, but one that was considerable and well known in the most civilised parts of the world. That of the Romans was the last, entirely extinct in the West, and of which only some feeble, miserable, and decaying remains are seen in the East. Notwithstanding, as if the Roman Empire had recovered its vitality and had begun a new life under our skies (which was far from being the case), this name, the greatest then in the memory of man, seemed alone to be worthy to distinguish and mark the pre-eminent position of Charlemagne ; and although this lofty height which he held only from God and his sword, of itself gave him sufficient right to take any title he chose, the Pope, who together with the whole Church was under the greatest obligations to him, was well pleased to contribute what he could to his glory, and to render more incontestable his quality as Emperor by a solemn coronation ; just as consecration, although it does not confer on us our royal position, does not fail to make it manifest to the people, and to render it more august, more inviolable, and more sacred. But this greatness of Charlemagne, who had so well founded the title of Emperor, or of still more magnificent names if they could have been found, did not endure long after him, being first diminished by the partition which took place at the time among the children of France, and subsequently by the feebleness and lack of wise care on the part of his descendants, in particular of that branch which had established itself beyond the Rhine. For Empires, my son, are only preserved as they have been acquired, that is to say, by vigour, watchfulness, and labour. The Germans, with the exception of the Princes of our blood, at once took possession of this dignity, or rather, substituted another in its place which had nothing in common either with the old Roman Empire or with the new Empire of our ancestors, but one in which they tried, as happens in all great changes, to make each one find it to his advantage not to oppose it. The different peoples and separate States gave their consent to it owing to the great privileges which were given to them in the name of liberty ; the Princes of Germany, because, from being hereditary as formerly, this dignity was made subject to election, and because thereby they acquired the right of nominating or aspiring to it, or both together ; and finally the Popes, because they always made profession of holding it by their authority, and because in reality a great and real Roman Emperor could be in a position to give himself a greater right over Rome itself than they (the Popes) might have wished. From which arises the fact that those who have searched most curiously into antiquity hold that Leo III, when he crowned him, did not attribute to Charlemagne the title of Emperor of the Romans which public acclamation gave to him subsequently, but only that of Emperor and Advocate of the Church and the Holy See ; for the word Advocate then signified Protector, and in this sense the Kings of Spain still qualified themselves a few years ago as Advocates of some of the towns in Flanders which I conquered, that country being almost entirely divided into different Advocateships or Protectorships of this kind.

But to come back to the Emperors of to-day. It is easy for you, my son, to understand from all that I have said that they are in no wise like what the former Roman Emperors were, nor like what our ancestors had been. For to do them justice one should regard them only as Chiefs and Captains-General of a German Republic somewhat new in comparison with several other States, and neither so great nor so powerful as to give it any right to superiority over neighbouring nations. Their most important resolutions are submitted to the deliberations of the States of the Empire ; when electing them they impose what conditions they will ; the majority of the members making up the Republic, that is to say, some Princes and the free cities of Germany, only give as much deference to their commands as they please. As Emperors under these conditions they have only very small revenues, and if they did not possess in their own right other hereditary Estates they would be reduced to having no other seat in the whole Empire but the one city of Bamberg alone, which the Bishop who is its Sovereign Lord is obliged to give up to them in such an event. In addition, several Princes, who might have

attained to this dignity by election, have had no desire
to do so, esteeming it to be more burdensome than
honorific ; and in my own time the Elector of Bavaria
could have been Emperor if he had not refused to nominate himself as the laws permitted, by adding his vote to
those I had assured on his behalf in the College of
Electors, and which I offered him.[41]

I do not see therefore, my son, by what reason Kings
of France, hereditary Kings, who can pride themselves
that there is not to-day in the world without any exception a better House than theirs, nor a monarchy as old,
nor a power that is greater, nor authority more absolute,
should be inferior to these elective Princes. We must
not disguise, however, that the Popes, in pursuance
of what they had already done, have insensibly given
precedence to the Ambassadors of the Emperor over
those of all others, and that the greater part of the Courts
of Christendom have imitated this example, without
our predecessors having made any effort to prevent it ;
but in all other matters they have defended their rights.
From the time of the tenth century [42] we find public
treaties wherein they place their names first before those
of the Emperors with whom they are treating ; and at
the Porte of the Sultan of Turkey our Ambassadors,
and, to mention him last, the Marquis de Brèves under
my ancestor Henry the Great not only disputed but
gained the precedence over those of the Emperors. In
a word, my son, just as I have not thought it my duty
to demand anything new from Christendom in this
matter, I have thought it still less so, considering my position, to put up with any fresh condition from the worldly
point of view whereby these Princes might presume to
claim the least advantage over me. And I counsel you
to observe the same attitude, remarking, however, how

greatly virtue is to be esteemed, since after so many centuries that of the Romans, of the first two Cæsars, and of Charlemagne still makes men render to it more honour, in spite of the real reason, than is properly due to the empty name and empty shadow of their Empire.

These trifling disputes with the Emperor made me still more desirous of diminishing his credit in Germany, or any which the House of Austria had acquired there during the last two centuries ; and, being more accurately informed as to the disposition of their minds, I detached the Elector of Trèves from this Cabal, after negotiations lasting some months.43   He entered the Rhenish Alliance, that is to say, a powerful and considerable Party I had formed in the midst of the Empire on the pretext of maintaining the Treaty of Munster and peace in Germany.44

Ten imperial cities which this same Treaty had placed under my protection then swore the oath to me which they had always refused.45

In order to establish my conquests in these countries and in Flanders by uniting them more closely with my old States, inasmuch as I did not find occasion to follow the practice of the Greeks and Romans which consisted in dispatching colonies of their own native-born subjects to newly subjugated countries, I endeavoured to establish therein French customs.   I changed the plenary Councils into Presidial Courts ;   I caused appeals from them to come before my Parliaments.   I put Frenchmen into the highest posts and, as far as I could, men of merit.   I wrote to the Generals of Religious Orders so that they might unite the Religious Houses of these countries to the old provinces of France.   I prevented the Churches in Artois and Hainault from continuing to receive rescripts from Rome through the intermediary of the

Inter-Nuncio in Flanders, and no longer permitted the Abbots of the three Bishoprics of Metz, Toul, and Verdun to be elected without my nomination, but signified my pleasure that whenever a vacancy occurred three candidates should be presented from whom I promised to agree upon one.

I had accorded my protection to Prince d'Epinoi during the war.⁴⁶ I put him in possession of the lands of the Comte de Buquoi until his own should be restored to him by the Spaniards as they had promised.

I delivered the Pays de l'Alleu,⁴⁷ which was at that time in dispute between them (the Spaniards) and me, from divers acts of oppression with which they were threatening them ; for on the pretext of certain arrears in the sum of twelve thousand *écus* which they had made a practice of levying, they had imprisoned twelve of the principal inhabitants, and had already exacted from them, on the score of expenses incurred, two thousand florins which I made them restore, together with their liberty, without consenting ever to listen to the harsh and ruinous expedients which Spain proposed to me for that country, namely to double the levy so long as our differences remained unsettled, so that both France and herself should each obtain our due.

In Artois I put a stop to certain levies which the city magistrates made under the pretext of city dues (*octrois*) allowed by the King of Spain.⁴⁸ In order to relieve the people I ordered the officers of the garrisons as well as the inhabitants to bear all the other taxes which were levied on food-stuffs. I allowed three years to the poor families on the frontiers whom their creditors had been pressing cruelly since the peace. I caused a large part of the boundaries to be marked out that year in execution of the Treaty of the Pyrénées, the fortifications of Nancy to be demolished, all my fortified cities to be repaired, placed in a state of defence, and supplied with all necessary things just as had been done in the midst of the war, fearing nothing so much as the reproach which had been brought against Frenchmen for so long a time, but which I hope to efface completely by my conduct, *videlicet* that they know how to conquer but do not know how to maintain their conquests.

I confess that in these beginnings, seeing my reputation increasing day by day, and everything becoming easy to me, and that I was succeeding, I was perhaps as much touched as I have ever been since by the desire to serve Him and to please Him.49

I gave authority to Cardinal Antoine and to Auberville, my Chargés d'Affaires in Rome, to form a League against the Turk, and offered to contribute with my money and my troops far more than any other of the Christian Princes.50 I gave a hundred thousand *écus* to the Venetians for their war in Candia, engaging to provide them with considerable forces each time they were desirous of making a fresh effort to drive the infidels from that island. I offered the Emperor an army of twenty thousand men against the common enemy, composed entirely of my own troops or those of my allies.51

I re-established by a new ordinance the rigour of former edicts against swearing and blasphemy, and determined that a few public examples should be made forthwith ; and I am able to say on this head that my care and the aversion I showed for this scandalous irregularity have not been without fruit, my Court being, by the grace of God, more free from it than for many centuries under the Kings, my predecessors.

I added new preventive measures against duelling to those which I had already enjoined ; and in order to show that neither rank nor birth could dispense any one, I banished from my Court the Comte de Soissons who had challenged the Duc de Navailles,[52] and put in the Bastille the man he had employed to be the bearer of his challenge, although the affair had come to nothing.

I applied myself to destroy Jansenism and to scatter the communities wherein this spirit of novelty was being fomented by men well intentioned perhaps but who were not alive to, or who wished to ignore, the dangerous consequences it might have.[53]

I made several interventions with the Dutch on behalf of the Catholics of Gueldres.

I gave orders that a considerable sum in alms should be distributed to the poor of Dunkerque, fearing that their poverty might tempt them to follow the religion of the English, to whom the Spanish War had compelled me to give this place during the administration of Cardinal Mazarin.[54] And as regards the large number of my subjects belonging to the so-called reformed religion, which is an evil which I have always regarded and still regard with much pain, I formed from that moment the plan of my whole conduct towards them, which I have no reason to think was a bad one, since God has willed that it has been followed, and is still being followed daily, by a very great number of conversions.

It seemed to me, my son, that those who wished to employ extreme and violent remedies did not understand the nature of this evil, caused partly by the heat of men's minds which it is necessary to allow to pass away and extinguish itself gradually rather than rekindle it anew by forcible contradiction, especially when the corruption is not limited to a certain known number, but is spread all over the State.[55]

As far as I have been able to understand the matter up

till now, the ignorance of the ecclesiastics in the preceding century, their luxury, dissoluteness, the bad example they gave, which they were consequently obliged to tolerate in others, and the abuses which they permitted in the lives of individuals contrary to the regulations and public sentiments of the Church, occasioned more than anything else the grievous wounds which she received through schism and heresy. The new reformers manifestly spoke the truth in regard to many matters of this kind which they rebuked with as much justice as bitterness ; on the, other hand, they were mistaken in all things which had reference not to fact but to belief. But it is not in the power of the people to distinguish a falsity when it is well disguised and otherwise lies concealed in the midst of several evident truths. A beginning is made with small differences, of which I have learnt that neither the Protestants of Germany nor the Huguenots of France take any practical account to-day. These engender greater differences principally because people press too hardly on some violent and bold man who, no longer seeing any honest retreat open to him, plunges deeper into the conflict, and, abandoning himself to his own interpretation, takes the liberty of probing into all that he had formerly imbibed. He promises the world an easy and shortened road to salvation—a method very suitable for flattering the human mind and drawing away the multitude. The love of novelty had seduced many. Divers interests of Princes were mixed up in this quarrel. The wars in Germany, and afterwards in France, redoubled the animosity of the baser disposed ; still less had the common people any doubts as to the goodness of religion for which they were exposed to so many perils. Fathers were deeply concerned over this question and passed it on to their children in the most violent form possible. But at bottom it is of the same nature as all other passions which time always tempers, and often with all the greater success when less effort is made to combat them.

In consideration of these general views I thought, my son, that the best means whereby to reduce the Huguenots in my kingdom little by little was not to press them at all by introducing any fresh rigour, and to respect the concessions they had obtained in preceding reigns, but at the same time to accord them no fresh ones, and to confine their observance within the strictest interpretation permitted by justice and decency. To this end I nominated this same year Commissioners to carry out the Edict of Nantes. I took pains to put down everywhere the activities of the adherents of this religion in places such as the Faubourg Saint-Germain, where I learnt that they were beginning to form secret assemblies and schools for their sect ; at Jamets in Lorraine, where, although they had no right of assembly, they had taken refuge in large numbers during the disorders of the war, and were there practising their exercises ; at La Rochelle, to which place they had drawn by degrees a quantity of others whom I compelled to depart, although permission to live there had only been given to the old inhabitants and their families.

But as regards those favours which depended on myself alone, I determined, and this I have observed very punctiliously since, to accord none to those of this religion, and this from kindness of heart and not from harshness, in order to oblige them thereby to consider from time to time, of themselves and unconstrainedly, whether it was for a good reason that they deprived themselves voluntarily of the advantages which they might enjoy in common with my other subjects.

In order that they might profit, however, by the state in which they found themselves, and might listen the more willingly to what might undeceive them, I also resolved, even by means of rewards, to draw those who should become docile, to rouse the Bishops as far as in me lay to work for their enlightenment and to remove from their own body the scandals which sometimes separated them from us ; to place no one in these high places, nor in any other to which I have the power of nomination, except men of piety, application, and knowledge, men able to repair by altogether different conduct the disorders which that of their former predecessors had in large measure caused in the Church.

But there are still many things, my son, which I have in mind to employ to bring back by every means those whose birth, education, and more often than not, a great zeal without knowledge, hold in these pernicious errors in good faith. And thus I shall hope to have other occasions of speaking of them to you in continuing these Memoirs, without explaining beforehand plans to which time and circumstances may bring a thousand changes.

I took all these pains from real gratitude for the favours I was receiving daily. But I perceived at the same time that they served me greatly in preserving the affection of my people, who were well pleased to see that though beyond comparison I was much more occupied than formerly, as regards my religious practices I was continuing to live in the same regularity in which the Queen, my Mother, had had me brought up, and they were particularly edified that year at my making the Stations of a Jubilee on foot, together with all my household, a matter which I did not consider should even have been noticed.

And to speak truly to you, my son, we are wanting not

only in gratitude and a sense of justice, but also in prudence and good sense, when we fail in veneration of Him of Whom we are only the lieutenants. Our submission to Him is the law and example of what is due to us. Armies, Councils, and all human activities would be a weak means of maintaining us on the throne if everyone thought he had an equal right to it with ourselves, and did not reverence a Higher Power of which our own is a portion. The public respect which we render to this Invisible Power might, in fact, be justly called the foremost and most important part of our polity had it not a nobler and more disinterested motive as a duty.

Take great heed, my son, I conjure you, not to have only this interested view as regards religion, which is very bad when it is the only one, and would not advantage you besides, because pretence always proves itself to be false and does not produce for long the same effects as truth. All the advantages over other men in the position we hold are undoubtedly so many fresh reasons for subjecting ourselves to Him who has given them. But towards Him exterior without inner observance is nothing at all, and serves rather to offend Him than to please Him. Form your own judgment of this, my son, if ever you find yourself (as is difficult to avoid sometimes in the course of your life) in that condition which is so usual with Kings, and in which I have seen myself so often. My rebellious subjects, when they have had the audacity to take up arms against me, have caused me perhaps less indignation than have those in close proximity to my person, who were rendering me more dutiful service and greater assiduity than all the rest, while I was well informed that they were betraying me, and had for me neither real respect nor real affection in their hearts.

In order to keep alive this inner disposition which I desire above all things, and especially for you, it is useful, my son, from time to time to place before one's eyes the truths of which we are persuaded, but the clear image of which our occupations, our pleasures, even our lofty position, continually efface from our minds.

It is not for me to play the theologian with you. I have taken extreme care to choose for your education those whom I believed most suited to instil piety into you by word and example, and I can assure you that this is the first quality that I looked for and considered in them. They will not be wanting, and I shall take care of that, in confirming you in good maxims, and more and more every day that you prove yourself capable of reasoning with them.[56]

Several of my ancestors have waited until the end of their life to give exhortations such as these to their children. I have thought, on the contrary, that they would have more force and greater weight with you while the full vigour of my life, the freedom of my mind, and the flourishing state of my affairs, would not permit of your suspecting any dissimulation in them or attributing them to any outlook due to fear. Do not give me this grief, my son, that they shall only have served to render you more blameworthy, as undoubtedly they will if you come to forget them.

THE DEATH OF THE KING OF SPAIN 57 and the war of the English against the United Provinces,58 occurring almost at the same time, offered me two important occasions for engaging in war simultaneously, the one against Spain in pursuance of the rights which were due to me, and the other against England in defence of the Dutch.

Not that the King of Great Britain did not provide me with a pretext sufficiently plausible to set me free of the latter quarrel by saying that in the Treaty which bound me to the Dutch I had only promised my assistance in the case of their being attacked, and that for this reason I did not owe them any help in this matter, in which they were the aggressors.

But although it would have been very convenient to me to have allowed myself to be persuaded to this view, I was anxious to act in good faith in pursuance of the terms of my Treaty, since I knew in reality that the aggression had come from England.

I delayed, however, as much as I could before declaring myself, in an attempt to reconcile them, but as my efforts were unfruitful, and I feared that the two parties might end by coming to an agreement by themselves to my prejudice, I determined to take the side to which my word had been given.

But this question disposed of, there was still another

which it was more difficult to decide, namely, to know whether I should enter into war with both England and Spain simultaneously so as to keep together my own interests and those of my allies, or if I should put off till another time my own quarrel, and only take in hand that of the Dutch first—undoubtedly an important matter to consider, from the number and weight of the reasons which might be advanced on both sides.

On the one hand I regarded with pleasure the idea of these two wars, as some vast field whereon each moment grand opportunities might arise of distinguishing myself. I saw so many brave men around me eager to serve, who appeared all the time to be begging me to provide them with some outlet for their valour which would be at greater advantage than in a war on the sea in which the most courageous have scant opportunity to distinguish themselves from the feeblest. But in my own interests I reflected that as the good of the State did not allow a King to expose himself to the caprice of the sea, I should be obliged to entrust to my lieutenants the entire fate of my arms without ever being able to act in my own capacity ; that, besides, inasmuch as I should be obliged in any event to maintain large forces, it would be more expedient to throw them upon the Low Countries than to feed them at my expense, and that, in addition, the entire House of Austria, fully alive to my intentions, would not fail to injure me indirectly wherever they could ; that, given the necessity of going to war, it was better worth my while to undertake one in which some visible gain could be seen, than to employ my efforts against islanders over whom I could never make any conquests that would not be more burdensome than profitable ; that if I undertook these two affairs simultaneously, the Dutch in their need of my aid against the English would be of more service to me against the Spaniards, instead of which, if they were entirely outside all danger, they might fear perhaps an increase of my power more than they would remember the benefits received from me ; and lastly, that several of my predecessors had found themselves in situations quite as important as this was likely to be, and that if I refused to expose myself to difficulties they had surmounted I should be in danger of not winning the applause they had merited.

But in support of the opposite point of view I observed that, just as a Prince wins glory by overcoming difficulties he cannot avoid, so he incurs the risk of being accused of imprudence by throwing himself too lightly into those from which a little address might have spared him ; that the greatness of our courage ought not to make us neglect the aid of our reason, and that the more dearly one loves glory, the more should one endeavour to win it surely ; that under the pretext of the war with England I should so dispose of my forces and of my information as to make a more favourable beginning in Flanders ; that the English by themselves need not be feared, but that their support would be of great weight in defending the territories belonging to Spain ; that to attack these two powerful enemies simultaneously would be to form between them a *liaison* which could not be dissolved when I wished, and would infallibly compel me either to continue to fight them both at once, or to settle my differences with them under less advantageous conditions ; that a union between Spain and England would promote the peace of Portugal ; 59 that, taking into consideration the present temper of the Dutch and their readiness to defend themselves, their help could not procure me as great advantages as the English could do me harm, and in my wish to take the future into consideration there was no more upright method of securing them in my interests than to allow my good faith to be visible to them by beginning the war solely on their behalf ; but that at least I should appear glorious in the eyes of all the nations of the earth if, having my own rights to follow up on one side, and on the other, to protect my allies, I could show myself capable of neglecting my own interests to undertake the defence of those of others.

I was for some little time divided between these two views. But if the first flattered my mood more agreeably, the second touched my reason with greater force ; and I felt that in the position in which I was situated I ought to do violence to my sentiments in order to attach myself to the interests of my Crown.

So I determined to undertake only the war on the sea, and in order to wage this more advantageously I wished to have the King of Denmark on our side.

The advantage which I saw in this was that by closing to the English the entrance to the Baltic Sea by his means, they would be deprived of all the commodities which they drew from it, and especially those things which were necessary on a voyage, and essential for conducting the war. The difficulty was that the Dutch, having quarrelled with that Prince, were demanding a certain sum to come to an agreement. But I arranged the matter by providing a portion of their claim from my own funds, and by means of this occasion I informed them in a secret Treaty of all the matters I required of them.

Meanwhile, I was gradually raising levies, and supplied my frontiers with troops and munitions. But the condition of Mardick was causing me disquiet.[60] For that place was at the time in a half-demolished condition, and I found it difficult to judge whether I ought to restore it with all diligence or complete its demolition. If I began repairing it I was afraid that my enemies would make a surprise attack before it was put in a perfect state of defence, and if I demolished it I was apprehensive that they might afterwards betake themselves there for the purpose of rebuilding it. But until I should make up my mind I stationed the Maréchal d'Aumont there with a small army corps.

I also felt some misgivings about the ships which were usually in the roadstead at Toulon. For, knowing that it was only defended by two towers very far apart, and that the English possessed pilots who knew those waters, I feared that they might take it into their heads to go there, and accordingly I sent Vivonne to concert with the Duc de Beaufort the proper measures to forestall this loss.[61]

The only thing remaining for me to do before opening the war was to consider how I should declare it. For, in accordance with my plan which I always had in view of finishing the war at the first encounter, I was well satisfied to act towards the English as honestly as might be.

With this intention I found means to contrive that the Queen of England, who was then in Paris,[62] should take upon herself to make the declaration, thinking only of paying her a compliment by doing so. For I merely begged her to testify to the King, her son, that owing to the singular esteem in which I held him, I could not without grief take this resolution to which I found myself bound by my word which I had given. And this appeared so straightforward to that Princess that not only did she charge herself with giving him notice of it, but even held that he ought to feel himself extremely obliged.

Meanwhile, after giving all orders necessary on

occasions such as this, I wished to make my resolve known to my subjects as well as to my enemies, and caused it to be published in the usual form.

But while I was getting ready my arms against England I did not forget to work against the House of Austria by every means that secret diplomacy could furnish. As I knew that the Portuguese war was like a kind of diseased intestine, the duration of which was infinitely weakening to Spain, I proposed to myself, with a view to keeping it up, to marry the King of Portugal to Mademoiselle de Nemours,[63] and sent Saint-Romain to that Prince to make the proposition, and to forestall all those which the Spaniards were continually making.[64]

On the side of Germany, Count Guillaume de Furstemberg had orders to work in concert with the Elector of Cologne and the Duke of Neubourg in order to persuade the Elector of Mayence, the Duke of Brunswick, and the other Princes close to the Rhine to unite with me in hindering the passage of the Emperor's troops into Flanders.[65] The reason I gave to them for this was that there was no other means of preserving peace in their country, nor of keeping my armies away.

To the same end I sent the Abbé de Gravel to reside privately at the Court of the Elector of Mayence and to observe his deportment from close at hand, because I well knew that it was not always sincere.

I also sent Pomponne at the same time to Sweden with orders to act as much for affairs in Poland as well as for those connected with the Low Countries.[66] For however it might be arranged I should have been well content to form some *liaison* with that State not so much for the purpose of helping me with their forces as of depriving my enemies of them.

I opened in addition secret relations with the Comte

de Serin to ftir up trouble in Hungary if I should go to war with the Emperor.⁶⁷

I had at my Court a Theatine Father who had been sent by the Duchess of Bavaria, with the knowledge of her husband, to make various propositions to me, and I was not altogether without hopes of detaching this Elector one day from the House of Auftria.⁶⁸

I gave ear also to what was proposed to me by the Electors of Mayence and Cologne touching the division of the States of the King of Spain which might be effected between the Emperor and myself in the event of that young Prince (Spain) dying. For although the matter did not appear very feasible in itself, I was desirous of allowing all the difficulties to be raised by the Emperor in order to let all the disappointment of the authors of this proposition fall upon him.

Dukes George William and John Frederick of Brunswick having fallen into disagreement, I thought it my duty to reconcile them, and caused Delombre, who was then returning from Poland to France, to work for this end.

I was also very glad to be chosen as arbitrator with the Crown of Sweden between the Elector of Mayence and the Palatinate in the dispute between them over the right of *vilfranc*,⁶⁹ but I would not consent to the Emperor, in the event of our opinions disagreeing, being nominated supreme arbiter, holding the view that although this could not arise but for the accident of this queftion, people might give another explanation of it.

In order to engage the Elector of Brandenburg to defend the States of Holland, I firft dispatched Dumoulin to him with proposals of a general kind, and then, desirous of putting the matter on a more precise basis, I decided to send d'Estrade, my Ambassador in Holland, but was obliged to countermand this on account of the refusal of the Elector to receive him. But although the arrogance of this Elector was very displeasing to me, I was not willing that it should be the cause of rupture of a Treaty which was advantageous to me and which was surrounded with many other difficulties besides, for I had to combat at that Court both the opinions of the Dowager Duchess and the influence of the Prince of Orange. But to a man who knows how to overcome himself there are few things which can withstand him. To arrange this matter I dispatched Colbert, *maître des requêtes*, and brought what I wished to a successful issue.⁷⁰ The Elector of Brandenburg undertook to maintain ten thousand men at his expense for the defence of the United Provinces.

From this example you may learn, my son, how essential it is for Princes to be masters of their angry feelings. On occasions of this kind which we can either dissimulate or take open notice of according to our choice, we should apply our minds not so much to consider the circumstances of the wrong we have received as to weigh the exigencies of the times in which we are living. When we become irritated unreasonably, it usually happens that while only thinking of wreaking our spite on him who has angered us we do harm to ourselves also. From the empty satisfaction we find in letting our vain anger break forth we often lose the opportunity of obtaining solid advantages. The heat which carries us away vanishes in a very little time, but the losses it has caused us remain always present to our mind, together with the grief of having occasioned them by our own fault.

I know better than any one how greatly the least things touching our dignity sensibly affect hearts which are jealous of their glory. But, nevertheless, reason does not wish that one should minutely take notice of everything, and perhaps it is also conformable to the elevation in which we are placed sometimes to neglect from noble motives what passes beneath us.

Exercising an altogether divine function here below, we ought to appear incapable of perturbations which might lower it. Or if it be true that our heart, in its inability to give the lie to the feebleness of its nature, still feels, in spite of itself, vulgar emotions taking rise in it, our reason at least should conceal them so soon as they are harmful to the public weal for which alone we were born.

We never arrive at the end of vast enterprises without undergoing divers difficulties, and if among them we find one which obliges us in outward appearance to unbend somewhat of our pride, the beauty which we hope from its success gives us sweet consolation within ourselves, and the brilliant results which are revealed in the end make glorious amends to us in the eyes of the public.

At the end of last year I had intended to create two hundred cornets of cavalry, but I only issued my commissions to one hundred and twenty, since I was only bound by the one war with England. I had also incorporated two hundred fresh companies of infantry in the old regiments in order that by gradually blending themselves with the others the number of my soldiers would increase without discipline becoming weakened, for I had already formed the opinion that the whole of the French infantry had not been very good up till then. And to render it better I caused part of the duties of the Colonels to devolve upon the young men of my Court, to whom I thought the wish to please me and the emulation they felt among themselves would give greater keenness.

With a view to removing from the different corps any sort of disagreement and jealousy I firſt regulated the disputes between them regarding their rank, which no one had ever dared to do before, and next I decided that each regiment of infantry should have twenty-four companies serving, while the others remained in garrison, each one to be drawn from in turn.

I had a plan to treat with the Duke of Brunswick for his troops in case I should require them. But as regards the Duke of Lorraine, although I was anxious to have his, I did not think it advisable to speak to him directly on the subject, knowing that he would wish to sell them to me for a high price, and on the condition that I kept them always together. But with the view of making him offer them himself unconditionally, I informed him that in pursuance of the terms of our Treaty I wished him to disband them, and this method did not fail to produce the result I had expected.

I also caused to be enrolled sixteen Swiss companies to enter the garrisons in place of the French ones I drew from them.

Further, to ensure throughout that all those who raised levies for me should acquit themselves as became their duty, I made them underſtand early that I would watch closely the manner in which they served me, and gave public notice that month by month I would review them myself.

The firſt review was appointed to be held at Breteuil on the 19th January. But I was prevented from going to it by a presentiment of the danger of the Queen, my Mother, which my love gave me, contrary to the opinion of the doctors.⁷¹

Although this event had been prepared by an illness of long duration it did not fail to touch me so sensibly as to render me incapable for several days of occupying myself with any other considerations than the loss I had sustained. For although I have told you straightforwardly that a Prince should sacrifice all his own movements to the good of his Empire, there are occasions when this maxim cannot be put into effect quite at once.

Nature had formed the first bonds which united me to the Queen, my Mother. But the links which are fashioned in the heart by the inter-relation of the qualities of the soul are broken much more hardly than those which are only produced by the intercourse due to blood alone. The energy with which that Princess had upheld my Crown during the period when as yet I could not act was evidence of her affection for me, and of her virtue, and the respect I rendered to her on my part did not at all consist in the simple duties required by convention. The custom I had formed of having her under the same roof with me, and even at the same table, and the care I took to see her several times each day despite the press of my affairs, were by no means a rule I imposed upon myself from reasons of State, but a mark of the pleasure I felt in her company. Her abandonment of sovereign authority which she had so fully given had made me know well enough that there was nothing for me to fear from her ambition, or to compel me to keep my hold over her by an insincere affectation of kindness.

Feeling unable after this misfortune to endure the sight of the place where it had occurred, I immediately left Paris and withdrew first to Versailles, where I could be more private, and a few days after to Saint-Germain.

The letters which I had to write on this occasion to all the Princes in Europe cost me more than might have been thought, and especially those to the Emperor,

and to the Kings of Spain and England, which seemliness
and relationship obliged me to execute with my own
hand.

I had her laſt wishes carefully carried out, except where
she had given inſtructions that no public ceremonies
should be rendered at her obsequies. For, finding no
other alleviation in the sadness caused by her death
than in the honours rendered to her memory, I gave
orders that everything which she herself had had carried
out at the death of the late King, my Father, should be
followed on this occasion.

In connection with these ceremonies different disputes
arose, as is usual. But the one moſt hotly debated was
that between the clergy and Parliament. The matter
having been decided by me in favour of the clergy,
Parliament witnessed its celebration at the Church of
Saint Denis with so much vexation that they sent to me
a deputation of the Gens du Roi in order to spare themselves the same mortification at Notre Dame.⁷² I heard
them at Versailles, and remarked that Talon, who was
the spokesman, was in some difficulty towards the end
because he guessed well that it would not be agreeable
to me, having been charged to requeſt of me that Parliament might be excused from attending the ceremony.
But although this proposal displeased me, before giving
my reply I did not omit to go over all the points in his
speech more carefully than I had intended. And my
reason was that as I had already decided some other
matters in opposition to the views of that body, it was a
good thing to let them see that I made no decisions
before being fully prepared thereon beforehand, in order
that they might not do themselves the honour of thinking
that I made it my business to depreciate them. But
going back finally to their requeſt not to go to Notre

Dame, I told them positively that I wished them to be there, and in addition that no one must be missing. And in this I was punctiliously obeyed.

At the beginning of the year another occasion had arisen in which the same method of proceeding had been successful with me. Inasmuch as the decrees I had just had published, and especially the one regarding the lowering of the scale of fees, were not agreeable to a single one of the officials, the *Enquêtes* 73 demanded that the Chambers should assemble, and had promised themselves to be able indirectly, under some pretext or other, to re-enter into deliberation over this matter ; and I knew that the President, thinking to do me a great service, was carefully practising various delays as though the assembling of the Chambers had still anything dangerous about it.

But to show them that they counted for very little in my own mind, I myself ordered him to assemble Parliament and to inform it that I would not have them talking any longer of decrees which had been authorised in my presence, and to see to it that they did not venture to disobey me. For, to put it plainly, I wished to use this occasion to make a striking example of either the complete subordination of this Assembly or of my just severity in punishing it.

And, as a matter of fact, the obedience it showed in dispersing without having undertaken anything, was soon after imitated by the most distant Parliaments, and made people see that Assemblies of this kind are only a trouble to those who are in fear of them.

Among matters to be attended to occasioned by the death of the Queen, my Mother, I have not mentioned the division of her property, because neither I nor my brother troubled ourselves much about it. But perhaps

I should have given you the account of a conversation
I had with him during the acuteſt ſtage of our common
grief, in which, after the moſt moving expressions of
affeƈtion which we gave to one another, I promised him
to extend my own to his children and to have his son
educated with you.74

For although the occasion when I said these things to
him, and my ſtate of mind at the time, left no reason
to doubt that they were only suggeſted to me by a purely
friendly feeling, it is, however, certain that when I had
thought over this conversation in full liberty of spirit
I could imagine no more delicate method of doing
honour to my brother, for which he would be beholden
to me, and at the same time of obtaining the moſt precious
pledge he could give as surety for his conduƈt.

I do not know whether it was this mark of affeƈtion
which gave occasion to his asking me a few days afterwards that his wife,* when in the presence of the Queen,
might have a chair with a back to it. As far as I was
concerned, I should have liked well never to refuse him
anything. But in view of the consequences all I could
do was to let him underſtand that everything that could
help to raise him above my other subjeƈts I would
gladly do, but that I did not think I could grant him
a privilege that would seem to liken him to me, pointing
out to him, from the considerations I muſt preserve to
my own rank, the novelty of his claim, and how unprofitable it would be for him to persiſt in it.

But all that I could say to him did not satisfy in any
way either his own mind or my sister's. They
even alleged that the Queen, my Mother, when dying
had made this requeſt of me, although as a matter
of faƈt she had not mentioned a word of it to me and was

* Henrietta of England, daughter of Charles I and Henrietta of France.

not capable of doing so, having made it sufficiently clear by her actions how jealously those of our rank should maintain the dignity appertaining to it. But from that incident my brother assumed a certain manner towards me which might have made me fear something troublesome had I not been acquainted with the nature of his heart and of my own.

Notwithstanding, a month after, the unexpected death of the Prince de Conti provided him with a fresh pretension regarding the Governorship of Languedoc, principally based on the fact that my Uncle had formerly held it.75

But again I did not think it my duty to yield to him on this point, being persuaded that after the disorder we had seen so often in the kingdom it would be wanting in foresight and reason to place important governorships in the hands of the Sons of France who, for the good of the State, should never have any other retreat than the Court, nor any other position of security but in the heart of their brother. My Uncle's example, brought forward by my brother, confirmed my view ; and what had taken place during my minority compelled me to foresee with greater care what might come to pass during your own, if I were to fail you in this respect. However, my brother and sister, who did not enter into this line of reasoning, and who were perhaps further embittered by the remarks of certain busybodies, showed in various ways that they were dissatisfied at my refusal. But, for my part, without appearing to notice anything, I gave them time to recollect themselves. As a matter of fact, they recovered themselves soon after, and both asked my pardon for the heat they had shown.

During that time Saint-Romain had arrived in Portugal where, finding that an understanding between that Crown and Spain had reached an advanced state through

the mediation of the (Portuguese) Ambassador to England, he could not break it off without giving the Portuguese the hope that in addition to the aid I was furnishing
to them in the name of M. de Turenne, I should soon
place myself in a position to help them openly.[76] Whence
it arose that inasmuch as these proposals were infinitely
agreeable to them, they lost no opportunity afterwards
of pressing incessantly for their execution both by means
of Saint-Romain himself or through the (Portuguese)
Ambassador to England whom I had then at my Court.[77]
But not finding circumstances favourable to granting
them this satisfaction so soon, I worked day by day to
keep their hopes alive, without intending meanwhile
to break off the measures I had taken.

I had another matter in the North which was no easier
to disentangle. The King of Denmark, alarmed at the
preparations which the Swedes were making against
him, had sent to me Annibal Chestet, his Grand Treasurer,
to press me to declare myself in his favour ;[78] and the
States of Holland, very pleased to seize such a fine
opportunity of making me break with Sweden, made
repeated requests to me in favour of the King of Denmark,
while on the other hand the Swedes were representing
to me through Pomponne that seeing all their neighbours
in arms they could not be the only ones to remain
unarmed, and that they even had reasons compelling
them to make war on the King of Denmark in case he
should attack the King of England, and they begged me
not to think that in this action they were planning anything against my interests.

The conjuncture was assuredly a delicate one, for to
leave the Swedes at liberty to attack the King of Denmark
would be to deprive me of every advantage which I had
promised myself in treating with him, but to declare

myself against Sweden on that account would also
be to break too lightly with a nation whom I hoped soon
to be able to use in a more important affair.

That is why, without definitely granting either to one
or other party what they desired from me at the time,
I sought to discover a middle course, and was so successful that shortly after I drew from the Swedes an assurance
that they would make no attack upon Denmark.

Wherefore, one might fairly reasonably ask whether
a Prince does not require as much ability to protect
himself from the different claims of his allies as to resist
the attacks of his enemies.

In truth, any one taking into consideration the number
of desires, importunities, and murmurings to which
Kings are exposed, would marvel less at seeing some of
them agitated by such a tumult of cries, and would find
more worthy of esteem those who, in the midst of these
disturbances from without, preserve within themselves
that calm which is necessary to the perfect economy of
reason.

Force of character assuredly is required to keep always
the correct balance between so many people who are
striving to make it incline to their side. Out of the vast
number of neighbours surrounding us, of subjects who
are at our bidding, of men who pay their court to us,
of ministers and servants who give their counsel or
wait upon us, there is hardly one who has not already
formed in his mind some claim ; and as each one of them
is applying himself wholly to give an appearance of
justice to what he is seeking, it is not easy for the Prince
of himself, taken up as he is by so many other thoughts,
to exercise always a perfect discernment between what
is good and what is bad.

As regards this, it would be difficult to provide you

with sure rules for the diversity of subjects which daily present themselves. But there are, however, certain general maxims of which it is well that you should be informed.

The first is that if you preserve towards all a universal complaisance you cannot nevertheless satisfy everybody, because what contents one always vexes several others.

The second is that one must not judge of the equity of a claim by the earnestness with which it is urged, because passion and self-interest have naturally more impetuosity than reason.

The third is that those who are in closest contact with you, and those whose advice you seek concerning the claims of others, are the very people over whose own requests you must take the greatest thought, or must consult people who are not of the same degree as they, from fear lest by taking the views of one concerning another's affair (even though they be not friends to each other) they may each favour the other reciprocally, having in their minds that the indulgence received by their comrade would be a good precedent for their own.

And lastly, the fourth is that one must always consider the consequences attaching to the request preferred rather than the merits of the man who prefers it, because the public good should always be placed before the satisfying of individuals, and no King in the world is so powerful that he will not soon ruin his State if he be determined to grant their requests solely to men of merit.

I am aware that one invariably gives offence to those whom one refuses, and that many always impute to the bad temper or the bad taste of the sovereign every difficulty presented by their request. It is also true that one always gives pain to oneself by rejecting the prayer of others, and that it is naturally pleasanter to draw gratitude to oneself than complaints. But in this matter, my son, we are obliged to sacrifice ourselves to the general welfare, and what is most vexing in this sacrifice is that although it costs us much it is little appreciated as a rule.

For, in reality, the greater number of those who distribute praise to Princes only set value on those virtues which are useful to them. The *beaux esprits* by profession have not always *belles âmes*, and in the (*belles choses*) which they utter in public they rarely refuse to take care of their own particular interests.[79]

While I was busying myself day by day over the defence of the States of Holland, I learnt that they still had their Ambassador in London, and with good reason suspecting their faith I desired them to recall him and give me a formal promise that they would make no arrangements without my participation.

In order to obtain a still stronger assurance of their fidelity I worked to gain credit in their counsels and to remove from their public places the partisans of the House of Orange who were always bound up with the English. And to this end I distributed money to several of their deputies.

Meanwhile the troops [80] I had introduced into Germany to assist them (although ill satisfied with the treatment they were receiving) were living there in the most disciplined manner, and in various ways were doing much by their conduct and energy. Even Spain, although previously she had had no part in this quarrel, had proof of their valour to her own hurt. For the secret purpose which she always had of opposing France led her to embrace the cause of the Bishop of Munster ; she wished to give him the opportunity of surprising two strong positions, Dalem and Willemstat, which were near their frontiers, and, in order that that Prince (the Bishop of Munſter) should give no alarm to the Dutch by sending troops there, she devised a scheme for providing them on the spot, by disbanding two regiments in the neareſt garrisons they had, which were forthwith placed in the pay of the Bishop. But this plot was entirely fruſtrated through the vigilance of my chiefs who had word of it and surprised and defeated the two Spanish regiments.

Several similar encounters, which it would be wearisome to relate here, forced the enemy to remain shut up, and by taking from them the liberty of the open country, caused them so great inconvenience that the Bishop of Munſter sent to me with offers of peace. But I would liſten to no proposal, and firmly relegated the arrangements of the matter to the Dutch because they had moſt intereſt in it. I employed the same procedure with them in regard to England. For the Ambassador whom the King of Portugal maintained at the Court of the King of England, having come on other matters to my Court, was making various overtures towards an agreement to which I would never liſten without the participation of the States.

In this respeƈt I can say that I preserved a fidelity towards them which perhaps they would not have kept under similar conditions towards me, for it goes without saying that in the plans which I had formed, either of these arrangements was very advantageous to me ; by making peace with the English I could save all the expense of sea forces and maintain larger forces on land, and by coming to an underſtanding with the Bishop of Munſter I was enabled not only to withdraw the forces which I had sent againſt him, but could make myself sure of his own which that Prince was offering me with all insiſtence.

Meanwhile, being advised that the English had entered

the Mediterranean Sea, I gave orders to my Admiral, the Duc de Beaufort, to take steps to go and drive them out as soon as possible.[81] Owing to the multiplicity of things required in the equipment of ships, he spent some months over it.

This delay did not fail to give the English a great opinion of their power, and to make them show great impatience to see my men on the sea so as to fight them. But from the moment the Duc de Beaufort had come out they did not appear to be so valiant, and found it suited them better to depart from those seas rather than to await him.

I might have contented myself with having chased them off after all the bravado they had exhibited in that quarter. But I thought it would be a still finer thing to follow them up into the ocean. This was carried out with only thirty-two ships in view of all their coast while the English remained shut up in their ports without daring to come out until they had put in order all their forces.

At last they assembled in the month of June, and to the number of (46) ships took to the seas.[82] At that moment, however, my ships were far away because I had been obliged to send them to Portugal for reasons which you will see afterwards.

The Dutch weighed anchor at the same time as their enemies and against my own judgment disposed themselves to give battle. For my ships were at a distance, and I remonstrated with them that they ought to await their return for two very important reasons, the first being that after joining our forces we should have so great an advantage over the English that victory could not fail us, and the second that in order to defeat them it would not even be necessary to fight the enemy, because, by merely leaving them to consume their provisions (which could not last long), they would be compelled to go back to their ports without any hope of revictualling themselves on account of the length of time and the difficulties they would encounter in making levies on their people who were not inclined to obey, and therefore it was not acting prudently to chance a victory which delay would give us with certainty.

However, this advice was of no avail, for the Dutch, piqued by the desire to conquer without my aid, gave battle and won. But according to all appearances they ought to attribute this success to the immoderate confidence of their enemies rather than to their own forces. For in truth their fleet seemed to the English to be so contemptible that they thought nothing else was needed to assure their victory than to draw them on to battle. In this belief, Prince Robert [83] (Rupert) withdrew himself from the rest of the fleet with twenty-three of their finest ships under the pretext of going to meet mine, but in reality to give the Dutch the courage to stand firm before what remained of the enemy in front of them. The whole island was eagerly awaiting news of the battle, as of a victory already assured. The commanders had promised this positively, the King was quite confident, and the people were celebrating their triumph in advance. But the success was of quite a different kind to their presumptions, and after a battle lasting four days I had finally the satisfaction of seeing fortune choose the same side as I had done. I will not tell you how many men and ships were lost on both sides ; these circumstances you will learn from every other writer, and they are not of great utility. But, pausing upon what may be serviceable to you, I will remark that the vanity of the English in boasting too soon of a victory they did not obtain made them quite ridiculous by forcing them to light bonfires over the whole island as if they had really won—bonfires which in their presumptuous rejoicings only revealed too clearly to the whole world how bad were the conditions of that State. In consequence the King was compelled to rejoice over his own losses in order to preserve a little authority, and to keep his subjects in the dark, to prevent them rising in rebellion.

As regards the Dutch, I will make this observation to you, that although they had succeeded in their enterprise one should not conclude that they were right in undertaking it ; because in coming to a sane judgment upon our dispositions we must not always limit our attention to the issues, which are sometimes happy and sometimes unfortunate, according as it may please the God of Armies, but must make use of the lights which He has given us to do on every occasion what is most conformable to reason. And without seeking further confirmation of this view, you will see the same fleets fighting on the same principles that very year and meeting with an altogether different measure of success.

To understand what kept back my ships at that time, I must take you back to the marriage of the Queen of Portugal at the point where I left it last year.[84]

After various hindrances by the Spaniards, this matter was definitely decided upon at last. But those who had endeavoured to prevent the decision employed all manner of artifices to render still more distant its fulfilment. It was deferred several times.

Meanwhile I had engaged to lend eight of my finest ships, which I always kept in readiness, for the passage of this Princess. So when I caused the Duc de Beaufort to sail into the ocean in pursuit of the English although his forces were somewhat inconsiderable for this enterprise, I would not allow him to use these eight vessels, because the Portuguese Ambassador let me know that he was daily expecting an order to start. At last the affair was appointed for the month of June, and in order to avoid certain difficulties touching the ceremonies which might arise, it was decided that the marriage could only take place on my ships.

But there still remained in my mind an important difficulty over these same ships which were exposed to capture during the voyage by both the English and the Spaniards, because the English (especially on their return voyage) might account them as enemy ships, and the Spaniards could attack them by right of war, and even if they respected them as belonging to me they could seize them in virtue of a special Treaty under which we had agreed that all French vessels found within fifty miles of Portugal might be considered as lawful prizes.

It was easier to find an expedient as regards the English, for I caused the Queen of Portugal to obtain a passport by which not only were my ships secured, but I could also (if I had been disposed to use bad faith) have derived considerable advantage, because on the return journey, in the event of their being the weaker they need only show their passport, and as often as they found themselves the stronger they could attack the English.

But as regards the Spaniards the matter was more difficult ; and, not doubting that with their powerful interest in thwarting the marriage they would put forth their utmost efforts on this occasion, I could find no other way of placing matters on a secure footing than in sending my fleet to the mouth of the river at Lisbon to await the arrival and return of my ships.

While all these things were taking place the Spaniards continued their negotiations without relaxation to come to an agreement with Portugal, and I too employed all possible means to prevent this, now in the direction of the King of Portugal, and now in that of Great Britain, and with the Spaniards also.

When once this matter was ready to be concluded, it occurred to me, amongst other expedients, to propose to the Queen of Spain to accept me as her mediator with a view to the gaining of a few days.[85] But contrary to what I had hoped, the proposition was accepted, and the Archbishop of Embrun,[86] after I had instructed him in what guise he might present it so as to render it plausible, obtained the consent of that Princess. It is true that afterwards she did not wish to remember it, and recognising after the event how lightly she had engaged herself, was reduced to the necessity of a disavowal.

All the world is agreed, my son, that there is nothing more dishonest than to go back upon what one has undertaken. But you should know that the sole means of keeping one's word inviolate is never to give it without mature thought.

Imprudence nearly always brings in its train repentance and broken faith, and every man who is capable of binding himself without good reason, in a little while becomes capable of eating his words without shame.

To deliberate at leisure on all important matters, and to take the advice of different people thereon, is not (as the foolish imagine) an indication of weakness or dependence, but rather of prudence and steadfastness. It is a surprising maxim, but one that is nevertheless true, that those who, in order to show themselves masters of their own conduct, are unwilling to take counsel in anything they do, hardly ever do anything that they wish. And the reason is that from the moment they unfold to the light of day their badly digested resolves, they find therein so many great obstacles and so many absurdities

that they are conſtrained to withdraw them, thereby
juſtly acquiring the reputation of weakness and incapacity
through those very channels whereby they had thought
to safeguard themselves.

The advice given us does not bind us to follow it,
except in so far as it seems reasonable ; and, far from
diminishing the proper sense of our own capabilities,
it draws attention to it more surely than anything else,
because all men of good sense are agreed that all the
good that is done or proposed in the adminiſtration
of the State muſt principally go to the credit of the Prince,
and that there is nothing which brings his skill into better
relief than when he knows how to secure good service
and good counsel from his principal miniſters.

There is this difference between the wise and imprudent
monarch, that the latter will nearly always be badly served
by the very people who pass for the moſt upright in the
world, while the former will very often know how to
obtain good service and good advice even from men whose
integrity might be moſt open to suspicion.

For in reality, in everything which refers to the conduct
of men one can eſtablish a general principle that all
have some secret leaning to their own particular advantage
and that the virtue of the moſt upright people is with
difficulty able to guard them againſt this natural movement if it be not sometimes supported by fear or hope.
Even if some one exempt from this general rule be met, it
is so singular a piece of good fortune that prudence does
not allow one ever fully to be assured that he has really
been found.

Considering things in this light according to their
usual course, which makes men shun what is bad and
seek after what is good according as they fear or hope,
it is certain that an imprudent Prince who does not know

how to bring all these great resources into play, and who listens to and treats equally all who are engaged in his affairs, almoſt as a natural consequence allows those very people who had applied themselves with the beſt intentions in the world to deteriorate in his service, because, as there is nothing to push them forward or to hold them back, they insensibly become slack or zealous according as their mood or intereſt dictates, scarcely ever giving a moment's reflection to their own conduct.

Inſtead, the moſt eager and the moſt intereſted in the service of an intelligent Prince dare not ſtray, however slightly, from the path they should keep, because they see him ever watchful over their actions, and fear, at the leaſt deviation, to lose the eſteem and truſt which are always their firſt intereſt. They do not permit themselves any licence because they know that no fault will be hidden from him ; they spare themselves in nothing because they are persuaded that no merit will fail to obtain the approval which is due to them in his sight. In a word, they carry out and advise always what they think is beſt because they are convinced that the favour, credit, and promotion to which they aspire, are only given in proportion to the zeal and fidelity which each one displays.

In order to continue the former cuſtom practised by my predecessors of keeping an Ambassador in Turkey, I selected La Haye to go to that Court.[87] He was the son of the previous Ambassador, who undoubtedly underſtood better than any other the manners of that nation with which he had had relations for a long time under his father.

But a private feud which had arisen between him and the then Grand Vizier, rendered the presence of that miniſter very damaging to my affairs. For it had happened that the Grand Vizier, when leaving his poſt

to his son, had bequeathed to him also all his hatred ;
so that when La Haye (fils) arrived on the spot he found
as his chief enemy the very man with whom he had to
conduct every negotiation.

He realised the effect from the moment of his arrival,
in the obstinate refusal to accord him the same treatment
which an Ambassador of the Emperor had quite recently
received. For, besides being almost the absolute master
in everything, the Grand Vizier had in addition taken
care to prejudice the Sultan against La Haye by informing
him that it was through the instigation of that minister
that I had permitted French corsairs to interrupt the
commerce of the Archipelago by raids.

La Haye, piqued by this refusal and wishing to clear
the matter up at his first audience, received no satisfaction. He felt so much annoyance at seeing his private
quarrel causing prejudice to my interests, that not only
did he protest that he would retire to my Court, but
abruptly threw down the capitulations he was holding
rolled up, by the side of the Grand Vizier, who alleged
that he had been struck by them.

Those who know that this Prime Minister exercises
in public on his own authority all sovereign power, and
receives all the honour paid to the sovereign, will not
doubt that he considered himself terribly insulted by
this act, both on account of the deference due to his
Prince, whose seal had been thrown to the ground,
and in his own person against whom the blow had been
struck.

He therefore caused La Haye to be detained as it were
a prisoner in the palace where this act had taken place.
But afterwards, taking into consideration the character
of Ambassador wherewith this man was honoured, and
the resentment which I might feel at the treatment

he had given him, he showed some vexation at the part he had taken in this affair. Already, as a matter of fact, the people of Constantinople were saying openly that he was in the wrong, and those at the Porte who were not favourably disposed towards him alleged that it was bad policy to have been willing to make an enemy of such an one as myself, on account of his private quarrels.

These considerations induced him to seek various channels whereby to smooth the matter over ; the first that he essayed was to tempt the Marquis de Guitry, the Master of my Wardrobe (who had gone to Constantinople out of pure curiosity) to assume the duties of Ambassador, offering to treat him in all respects as he could desire. But when he found that he was not disposed to take upon himself such a matter without orders, he begged the Chief Pasha, one of his nearest relations, to mollify La Haye with polite words, after which he himself paid him all the honours he had at first disputed, and, in excuse for his behaviour, also wrote to me that he had arrested La Haye in his palace only from fear that that minister, carried away by his mortification, would withdraw forthwith from the Porte and would come to me with a report other than the truth. This was undoubtedly very remarkable amends, in view of the procedure of that nation which very rarely unbends in matters to which it has once set its hand.

Another incident occurred at that Court with which I was not satisfied. The Genoese (departing from the ancient custom of all Christendom which had only traded with the Turks under the Flag of France) had sent envoys to the Porte from their head and claimed the right to traffic with them under their own flag. I had charged La Haye to protest against this in my name, but the bad odour in which he was held by that Court prevented my hoping for the satisfaction I might have had. I determined to obtain this from the Genoese themselves when I had leisure to go into this matter seriously with them.

That same year I also had an affair with the Iroquois, the barbarian nation in Canada.[88] But matters succeeded more favourably for me there, for the troops which I had dispatched to that region executed three separate marches in this one campaign, each of over three hundred leagues, through places which were absolutely uninhabited, where it was necessary to march all day over snow and to lie out in the open all night. So the barbarians, surprised in their own settlements, saw them laid waste without hope of relief, and finding themselves despoiled of their grain, and even of several of their children whom my men took away before their eyes, they humbled themselves before them with all possible submission and agreed to conditions of peace which in all probability will ensure for ever the tranquillity of my French colonies.

The inhabitants of Tunis, worn out by the continual alarms occasioned by my ships, desired to make peace with me, and the Algerians going further, offered me in addition their services against England.[89] I would not accept this last proposal. But over and above this, touched by the desire to obtain the freedom of so many Christian slaves whom those barbarians were keeping in chains, and of enabling all the faithful to trade in security under the Flag of France, I sent Dumoulin, who in a short while concluded treaties with both nations, under more advantageous conditions, than any other European Prince had ever obtained.

There occurred, however, an incident in connection

with the Treaty with Tunis which made its conclusion difficult. The King, with whom the articles had been arranged, was imprisoned following a revolt, and his enemies, who had assumed all authority in the administration of the republic, would doubtless have broken this agreement as they did as regards all the other acts made during the reign of that Prince, if terror of my arms had not obliged them to carry it out. The first fruits I drew from it was to see more than three thousand French slaves rescued from the hands of these unbelievers.

On this account I was held in such consideration in the Mediterranean Sea that the Spaniards, having to secure the passage of the Empress to Italy,⁹⁰ dared not undertake it without asking for a passport from me, which I straightway granted them with all the politeness with which I could accompany it. At the same time I gave orders to all my ports that in the event of the Empress being obliged to touch at them they should treat her with the same marks of respect as they would have rendered to myself. These orders, however, did not take effect, for the Empress arrived in Italy after a favourable voyage, but they were very efficacious in the case of seven Spanish galleys who, one day meeting Vivonne who was in command of mine, refused to lower their standard at his command, and Vivonne, who was much the stronger in numbers and equipment and could have taken them without a fight, sent them on their way for the sole reason that they were carrying the wearing apparel of the Empress.

At the rejoicings which took place at Vienna on the occasion of her marriage, they took it amiss that the Chevalier de Gremonville, my Resident, had not put aside the mourning which he was wearing for the death of the Queen, my Mother. As soon as I was advised of this, although this marriage was not a very agreeable *fête* for me, I gave orders to Gremonville to leave off his mourning, and also sent him some money to increase his usual expenditure on this occasion.

In the meantime, I was negotiating at that Court an important affair for the Duc d'Enghien.91 Although the Queen of Poland had made over to him in his marriage settlement the Duchies of Oppeln and Ratibor, and no one could contest these *seigneuries* because they had been securely mortgaged to Sigismund Casimir by the Emperor Ferdinand, the Emperor had been unwilling, up till then, either to invest him with them or to repay him the sums for which they had been mortgaged. But as soon as the matter was handled in my name it was happily arranged ; and in return for these two domains, which only produced thirty-five thousand pounds of revenue for the Duc d'Enghien, the Emperor caused to be paid over to him in France sixteen hundred thousand pounds, without taking into account one hundred thousand *écus* which were left in the hands of his superintendent for having treated us so well and his master so ill, so that it cost that Prince nearly two million pounds.

Among corrupt ministers there are very few to be found so bold as openly to put their hands into their master's purse and appropriate directly the money over which he has given them the control, because that is a crime of which they could be too easily convicted. But the method of robbery which they find to be the most convenient, and which they believe to be safest against future investigation, is to take in another's name what they purpose to gain profit from for themselves. The wiles which they practise to this end are of so many different kinds that I will not undertake to explain them to you in detail. But I will only tell you that they all have this in common that they always go on augmenting the theft which they have endeavoured to conceal.

In reality there is no doubt that the individual whose services the minister wishes to use in gaining these kinds of profits would never enter into the business unless he found some advantage for himself ; and of necessity (under some form or another) the Prince, at whose expense this combination is arranged, bears at the same time both the burden of the unjust profit which his minister wishes to make and, in addition, the benefit to the other who provides the cover for this theft.

It is certain, furthermore, that in all these fraudulent conspiracies there are none which so much harms the Prince who suffers them as those in which foreigners are concerned, not only because the loss falls entirely on his own State, but also because it ruins his reputation with his neighbours, who recognise only too clearly by proofs such as these how little care or intelligence he gives to his affairs.

This consideration alone should, in my opinion, render more circumspect the unfaithful servants who carry on transactions of this kind, and at least it should teach their masters to be not content with examining men before taking them into their service, because the majority can easily disguise themselves for a time in view of attaining the authority they set before themselves, but also observe them still more carefully when they are actually in the management of affairs because, being then in the enjoyment of what they wish, they often follow their evil inclinations with greater freedom, the effect of which always falls upon the conduct of affairs or upon the reputation of their masters.

Such continual watchfulness will enable the Prince, by recognising accurately the weak spot in all who serve him, either to correct them with good advice according to their different characters, or to remove them when they are incorrigible, or even (if they have otherwise qualities to justify his putting up with them) to safeguard himself from the harm which their failings might do to his affairs, by taking pains to distinguish in their actions or proposals between what might be of good to his service and what proceeds from their evil propensities.

I continually divided my attention between home and foreign affairs. When I learnt from England and Germany that the plague still continued there, I applied myself to discover all possible precautions to prevent its being communicated to my States, and sent commissioners expressly to all the frontiers that were most under suspicion in order to have my orders carried out exactly.

But all my diligence could not prevent Graveline and Dunkerque from becoming infected, owing to the perpetual intercourse taking place between the different countries. In these unhappy circumstances I relieved by my care and from my own purse the families of the poor who were afflicted, and made use of every expedient I could think of to prevent this evil extending to neighbouring places. The one that I judged to be most efficacious was to augment considerably the pay of those garrisons infected with the plague, because, failing this, the soldiers who were not otherwise prevented from going out like the inhabitants, out of consideration of their goods and chattels and their families, might insensibly mingle with the crowd, and by associating with my other troops might have carried the infection to them.

But what appeared to me to demand the greatest precaution was the return of the troops which Pradelle was bringing back to me from Germany. And I prescribed so exactly all he had to carry out on the march in order not to bring us the infection that in the result the interior of my kingdom received no hurt.

I allowed no quarrel to arise between people of consideration which I did not at once settle, and I promoted as much as lay in my power the general rule I had determined to make of curtailing and cutting down lawsuits, in my resolve to comply with the wishes of the public as regards a large amount of this work.

Being advised that the people in several provinces were being ill-used by certain folk who were abusing the name of governor in order to make unlawful exactions, I established officials everywhere so as to be more accurately informed of such exactions, which I could punish subsequently as they deserved.

I also made a change in my household at that time, in which all the nobility of the realm had an interest. This had to do with my chief stables in which I increased the number of pages by more than half, and took pains both that the selection was made with more care and that they were better instructed than they had been up till then.

I was aware that what had prevented people of quality from aspiring to these kinds of positions was either the ease with which all conditions of folk had been recommended and admitted to them, or the scant opportunity afforded to them as a rule of approaching my person, or the neglect to perfect them in their duties which had insensibly arisen. To remedy all this I determined to take care to appoint all the pages myself, to make them share with those of my private stables all the domestic services which the latter rendered me, and to choose the best instructors in my realm to train them.

As regards the public, the results I hoped to obtain were to provide an excellent education for a large number of gentlemen, and for my own private benefit to have always a supply of people coming from this school more capable, and better disposed than the general run of my subjects, to enter my service.

I had yet another object for my personal attention which concerned principally people of substance, but the effect of which was afterwards spread over my kingdom generally. I knew what immense sums were spent by private individuals and were perpetually being withdrawn from the State by the trade in lace of foreign manufacture. I saw that the French were wanting neither in industry nor in the material for undertaking this work themselves, and I had no doubt that if they did this on the spot they could provide it far more cheaply than what they imported from such a distance. From these considerations I determined to establish works here, the effect of which would be that the great would moderate their expenditure, the people would derive the entire benefit of what the rich spent, and the large sums leaving the State would insensibly produce additional abundance and wealth by being retained in it, and beyond this would provide occupation for many of my subjects who up till then had been forced either to become slack through want of work or to go in search of it among our neighbours.

However, inasmuch as the most laudable plans are never carried out without opposition, I foresaw well that the lace merchants would oppose this with all their power, because I had no doubt that they found it paid them better to sell their wares which came from a distance, whereof the proper value could not be known, than those which were manufactured here within sight of everybody.

But I was determined to cut short by my authority all the trickery they might use, and so I gave them sufficient time to sell the foreign lace which they had before my ediĉt was published, and when this time had expired I caused all that they ſtill had to be seized as having come in since my prohibition, while, on the other hand, I caused shops filled with new manufactures to be opened, at which I obliged private individuals to make their purchases.

The example of this in a short while set up the manufacture of many other things in my State, such as sheets, glass, mirrors, silk stockings, and similar wares.

I took special pains to find out how to augment and assure to my subjeĉts their maritime trade by making the ports I possessed safer, and seeking places to conſtruĉt new ones. But while doing this I took in hand another enterprise of no lesser utility, which was to link by a canal the Ocean with the Mediterranean,⁹² in such wise that it would be no longer necessary to go round Spain to pass from one sea to the other. It was a great and difficult undertaking. But it was infinitely advantageous to my realm, which thus became the centre, and as it were the arbiter of the trade of the whole of Europe. And it was no less glorious for me who in the accomplishing of this objeĉt raised myself above the greateſt men of paſt centuries who had undertaken it without result.

Over and above my expenditure on these objeĉts and the others conneĉted with armaments on land and sea of which I have spoken, I was further obliged to incur much in a more secret manner in the negotiations I maintained with foreigners. There were several Dutch deputies who were in my pay. I also gave considerable sums to several *seigneurs* in Poland so as to make use of their votes at the election which was being considered ; I maintained pensioners in Ireland with the object of stirring up the Catholics against the English, and I entered into relations with certain refugees from England to whom I promised to furnish large sums to resuscitate the remnant of the Cromwell faction. I gave a hundred thousand *écus* to the King of Denmark to make him enter the league against the King of Great Britain, and after that presented a valuable necklace to the Queen, his wife. I had another sent to the Electress of Brandenburg and made a present of considerable value to the Queen of Sweden, not doubting that these Princesses (over and above the general interests of their States) would feel honoured in their persons by the pains I took to seek their friendship. Being aware of the credit which the Chancellor enjoyed in Sweden, and what power the Prince of Anhalt and the Comte de Schwerin had with the Elector of Brandenburg, I did what I could to win them over by my liberality.

For while, on the one hand, I was continually working to reduce minor superfluous expenses, as I did this year by cutting down the contributions raised for the soldiers, by suppressing the greater number of the war commissioners and by suspending my building operations, by,93 . . . on the other I also spared no sums for important things, especially the increasing of the number of my friends or diminishing that of my enemies, in view of the weighty designs over which I was continually pondering.

If it is truly advantageous, my son, for the Prince to know how to be prudent with his money when the peaceful state of his affairs allows him the liberty, it is no less important that he should know how to spend it, even somewhat profusely, when the needs of his State

require it or fortune offers him some special opportunity
of exalting himself above his equals.

Sovereigns, whom Heaven has made to be the deposi-
tories of the fortunes of the public, are certainly acting
in opposition to their duty when they scatter the substance
of their subjects in unprofitable expenditure, but they
are doing a still greater ill when by misplaced caution
they refuse to disburse what may contribute to the glory
of their nation, or the defence of their provinces.

It often happens that moderate sums dispensed at the
right time, and with judgment, save States incomparably
greater expenses and losses. Without any formal vote
which can be cheaply acquired, it is sometimes necessary
to levy large armies. A neighbour whom we could
have made our friend with little expense sometimes
costs us very dear when he becomes our enemy. The
smallest number of enemy troops who are able to make
a raid upon our States take from us in one month more
than would have been required for the maintenance of
secret intelligence service for ten years. And imprudent
economisers, who do not understand these maxims,
sooner or later meet with the punishment due to their
miserly conduct, in wasted provinces, in the cessation
of their revenues, in being abandoned by their allies, and
in the contempt of their people.

Why make a difficulty in spending money on public
necessities, since it is only to satisfy those needs that we
have the right to raise it ? To love money for money's
sake is a passion of which fine souls are not capable ;
they never consider it as the object of their desire, but
only as a necessary means to the execution of their designs.
The wise Prince and the miserly private individual are
absolutely opposed to each other in their conduct ;
the rich miser always seeks after money with avidity,

receives it with extreme pleasure, saves it up without discernment, guards it apprehensively, and cannot spend the smallest portion without unbearable grief ; whereas the virtuous Prince only imposes his levies with restraint, exacts them with compassion, uses them with a sense of duty, holds them in reserve only from prudence, and never spends them except with altogether peculiar satisfaction because he does this only to add to his glory, to increase his State, or to benefit his subjects.

Over and above the hundred thousand *écus* I had already provided in order to come to an arrangement with the King of Denmark, the Dutch wished to oblige me further to give a fresh sum to that Prince. And the reason for this demand was that they desired him to send his ships to the Channel to form a junction with our fleets, from which he excused himself by saying that he was only obliged by our Treaty to keep his ships in the Baltic Sea in order to close them to the trade of our enemies, but that, nevertheless, if we were willing to pay all the expenses of this passage, he would readily make this contribution to the common cause.

I replied to this proposition that after the great sums I had already disbursed for the States of Holland, both on the armaments on sea and land which I had got ready for their defence, and also on the King of Denmark's account, I felt I ought not to burden my subjects with still greater expenditure.

From the moment I had resolved to declare war against the English I did not doubt that in the Southern Islands, where my subjects mingled with them, they would soon commence hostilities against each other ; 94 and in order to strengthen them for this eventuality I drew eight hundred men from the garrisons nearest the sea and sent them with all haste to their aid. But I learnt soon after that my wishes and my good luck were far in advance of the arrival of my ships. For news of the war having been carried to the Island of St. Christopher more speedily than might have been thought, and becoming known to both sides at once, my enemies, although beyond comparison stronger in numbers, were nevertheless beaten, contrary to their own opinion of themselves and to all likelihood.

Indeed, the French, who numbered only sixteen hundred in the whole Island, whereas there were at least six thousand English, at first suggested remaining at peace as heretofore. But they learnt that their enemies had resolved to put them all to the sword in accordance with an express order of their Viceroy, the original of which was afterwards found in the pocket of one of the dead.

However, this order so easy to give was not so easy to execute. For the French, aroused rather than cast down by the greatness of their peril, behaved with so much valour and diligence that after having given battle to different detachments of the enemy four times on one day, were everywhere victorious, and forced any enemies who escaped to abandon their forts and leave the Island, or to take an oath of fidelity to me.

At the same time the Thames was practically besieged by the victorious Dutch who for more than a month remained at the mouth while the King of Great Britain, urged on by the seditious murmurs of his whole Island, was labouring to put his fleet in order again.

At last he sent it to sea on the 95 . . . and with better fortune than the first time, for he defeated the Dutch fleet who were split up through the imprudence of Vice-Admiral Tromp, the disgrace of which caused a dangerous dispute among the Dutch. For though in reality that Captain had not separated without the order of his

General of the Dutch Army Corps he had, besides, acquired such reputation by his valour and made it so clear that this plan which, from chance, had not succeeded, was based on good reasons, that he formed a powerful party in the States to defend him. The interest I then had in keeping this republic united made me use my authority to allay the dispute which was taking place.

As regards my fleet, it was then still at the mouth of the Tagus, awaiting always the arrival of the Queen of Portugal, for the voyage of this Princess was taking an unusually long time. Meanwhile the Dutch, cast down by their defeat, were urging me with continual insistence to bring up my ships, and in this matter they were favoured by fortune. For, inasmuch as it had been difficult to foresee the excessive duration of the voyage, the provisions of my fleet were used up, and as the Portuguese only offered to my Admiral supplies of very bad quality, necessity which overrides all orders and considerations, forced him to take his course back to France before the Princess whom he was awaiting had arrived.

Nevertheless, I represented his return to the Dutch as having been decided upon out of my consideration for them, and in fact I informed them first by express courier, in my desire to make him (the French Admiral) of service in their affairs. I then saw to it to keep ready in my ports vessels laden with all manner of stores to revictual my ships without stopping them, and changing the order I had given to halt at Belle-Isle or Brest, I commanded them to go on without stopping and join up with the Dutch, who had come out of their ports after recovering from their defeat.

Everything was carried out by my men with such good faith and punctiliousness that when the seven ships borrowed by the Queen of Portugal rejoined the rest of my fleet during its voyage, and found themselves without provisions of any kind, they preferred to draw from the others some of their stores rather than delay a moment to revictual themselves. Lastly, I exercised such foresight in order to facilitate the junction of our fleet that I adjusted by a private arrangement, consistent with the safety of the Admiral, all the difficulties which might have delayed it, and to ensure this I also issued secret orders of which my men availed themselves, as occasion arose, to put an end to any dispute which might still exist.

But in proportion as I acted with sincerity on my part I met with bad faith on that of the Dutch. As I believed that they would not fail to give battle before or after the junction, because the English and the Dutch were very close to each other, I had ordered my ships to go to Dieppe and embark six hundred armed men chosen from my household troops to give courage by their example to the rest of the crews. But immediately afterwards it was reported to me that the opposing fleets had drawn off without fighting, and that the English had gone and posted themselves at the Isle of Wight, which was directly facing our passage, and that the Dutch, instead of following them up or going to meet my ships as they had expressly stipulated to do by the pact regarding the junction, had retired towards their own country as though to give the opportunity to the enemy, who were three times stronger than I was, to defeat my fleet at their ease.

The Comte de la Feuillade, whom I sent first to remind them of their word and to show them the importance of this breach of faith, found them so little disposed to do what they had promised that instead of advancing to meet my ships they weighed anchor from Boulogne, where they were, in order to withdraw under his very eyes much closer to their own ports, and then Vilquier, the Captain of my Guard whom I sent for a like purpose, found them in the same mind. In this their behaviour is undoubtedly inexcusable, for whether this was from a purpose they had formed to abandon me at need, or that the illness of their General Ruyter had absolutely deprived them of the boldness to face their enemies, it was undoubtedly a breach of good faith, or very conspicuous cowardice.

You can imagine the disquiet my mind suffered during this time, for I knew that my ships were in the Channel, and whatever diligence I could use in sending out vessels from all my sea-board towns to scour the sea incessantly and report to my Admiral all that had happened, I was never able to warn him of the retreat of the Dutch, and was surprised to learn one day that he had arrived at Dieppe.

It was assuredly a cause for satisfaction to me that although he had passed in sight of the enemy, they had not had the boldness to attack him. But on the other hand I considered that in all likelihood when they had reflected on the advantages they possessed they would not fail to make use of them ; that I had no port on the Channel capable of putting my fleet under shelter ; that if it had the intention of going to join the Dutch at the spot to which they had retired it would be obliged to pass through the Pas-de-Calais where the English could arrive in shorter time ; and lastly, that if it decided to turn back towards Belle-Isle, which was the nearest shelter I could offer, it would still have to pass in sight of the Isle of Wight where we had left our enemies.

Not knowing how to resolve this difficulty, I left my Admiral at liberty to take his own part according to any information of the English he might obtain. But, although he could find out nothing for certain, my good fortune caused him to lean to the more prudent course; and while the enemy fleet went to meet him in the direction of Calais he turned back without danger towards Brittany ; whereas certain Dutch ships which up till then had been following mine in order to ensure their own safety, decided to separate and return to their own country, and were nearly all taken by the English fleet.

Only seven of my ships, which had kept far from the rest on the first passage, were in danger of being lost, but some of these discovered the enemy in time and evaded him. Others, becoming engaged, extricated themselves after exchanging cannon shots, and one alone, finding herself unable to escape, showed such an obstinate defence that she caused more damage to her captors than she brought profit to them.96

Meanwhile, the Portuguese marriage had taken place to the general satisfaction of the whole kingdom, and as the new Queen had acquired sufficient credit at that Court, I thought I should avail myself of it to combat the influence of the Comte de Castel Mayor, who, holding the first place in the councils of the King, his master, was seconding with all his power the plans of the King of Great Britain to reconcile the Portuguese with the Spaniards. That Princess, being informed of my intentions, followed them with such zeal that she soon quarrelled openly with the Comte.

The Queen of Poland 97 had no less affection for France, and would have well liked to let the tottering crown which she alone seemed to be sustaining by her virtue, fall on the head of a Prince of my House, but her affairs were then in such a bad state that it was not easy for her to succeed in this plan without powerful assistance. To this end I had decided at the beginning of this year to send the Prince de Condé to Poland with 500 horse and 6,000 foot-soldiers in the event of my affairs permitting it. But being constrained immediately afterwards to declare war against the King of England I did not feel myself any longer in a position to execute this project. Concerning this I promptly informed the Queen of Poland, sending her at the same time by way of consolation a sum of 200,000 pounds, which I had not led her to expect at all. This did not prevent her from dispatching a gentleman to my Court at the end of May to ask of me further assistance. Now, foreseeing clearly the difficulty which might arise over her request, she had given two different commissions to the man who came, one as a mere envoy under the pretext of paying me courtesy over the death of the Queen, my Mother, and the other as Ambassador Extraordinary charged to make the request of which I have just been speaking, and leaving the bearer at liberty to use one or the other in accordance with the hopes he might entertain of the success of his negotiations.

As soon as I was informed of these details I was anxious that the King of Poland should not cause a much talked of mission to be given public prominence, only to end in nothing. To ensure this I gave a hint to his minister to present himself to me only as an envoy ; but whether he wished to satisfy his own private vanity under a more eminent title, or wished to obtain thereby some other advantage for his King, he assumed, against my wishes, the quality of Ambassador.

I received him with all the customary honours, although at first I was determined to yield nothing of what he requested. But immediately afterwards I was unable to prevent myself from granting him a very important sum, for my Ambassador, the Bishop of Béziers, informed me that the Lithuanian army (which constituted all the strength and authority remaining to the King of Poland) was on the verge of mutiny, and that he had thought it to be his duty, even without my orders, to undertake to pay them a *quintal*, that is to say, a certain portion of their pay, and I judged that I ought not to disavow a promise given for so pressing a reason. This I also recognised from subsequent events, because the attachment which this army continued to show in the service of their Prince was the principal means which compelled the return of his rebellious subjects to the obedience they owed him.

At one of the conferences I held with the Ambassador over the affairs of that Kingdom, he took upon himself to ask me curtly whether I still desired to insist on the election as I had up till then, or if I had decided to waive it. The question was a delicate one in itself, but it seemed to become still more so from the manner in which it was made, for I had been good humouredly alive to the fact that he was a very difficult man, and thus I had cause to fear that if I persisted in the design of the election this disappointed man would make use of my answer to embroil me with the Polish States, who at that time were entirely averse to the matter ; and if I declared that I intended to desist from it, I saw that it would be the absolute renunciation of a claim to forward which I had already made moves and had incurred extremely heavy expenditure.

On this account, summoning all my intelligence to formulate a reply midway between these two extremes, I told him that in the present state of my affairs I was not at all thinking of pursuing my former design, and that it was necessary to wait until matters were more favourable before considering whether it were opportune to go back to our former views ; by which speech I thought I could not wound either the present mood of the Poles nor the expectations of France.

While on this incident I will take occasion to observe to you how important it is for Princes to carry the greater part of their own counsel in their own heads, and how momentous their words often are as regards the success or ruin of their affairs. For although I am continually speaking to you here of my conversations with foreign ministers, I shall not pretend to counsel all indifferently who wear crowns to put themselves to this proof without having examined carefully beforehand whether they are capable of emerging successfully therefrom. And I am of opinion that those of moderate genius act more honestly and more safely in abstaining from this function, than in being willing to display their feebleness before the eyes of their neighbours, and thus endanger the interests of their provinces.

Many monarchs would be capable of conducting themselves prudently in matters over which they had time to take counsel, who would not be equal to upholding their affairs by themselves in the face of skilful and experienced men, who never come to them unprepared, and who always seek to take advantage of their masters. Whatever notion of the subject to be treated may have been given to us, a foreign minister is able at any hour, either from chance or design, to propose certain things to us on which we are not prepared. And notwithstanding this, what is annoying is the fact that the false moves which the sovereign then makes can only be disowned by his acknowledging his incapacity, and they infallibly strike a blow either against the interests of his State or his own reputation.

But it is not only in important negotiations that a Prince must take heed of what he says. Even in the most ordinary conversation he is the more often in danger of failing. For he must guard himself well from thinking that because a sovereign has authority to do everything he also is at liberty to say everything. On the contrary, the greater and more highly considered he be, the more should he himself weigh what he says. Things which are of no account in the mouth of a private individual often become important from the sole reason that it is the Prince who has said them. Above all, the least mark of contempt he shows for a private individual cannot fail to do great harm to that man, because at the Courts of Princes every one is only esteemed by his fellows in proportion as they think he is esteemed by their master. And from this it happens that those who are offended in this way carry in their hearts, as a rule, a wound that only ceases with life.

There are two things which can console a man for stinging banter or a contemptuous word uttered by one of his fellows ; the first is when he promises himself to find an opportunity soon to return a similar one ; and the second is when he is able to persuade himself that what has been said to his disadvantage will not make an impression on those who heard it. But the man about whom the Prince has spoken feels his hurt all the more keenly because he has not any of these remedies. For if he dares to speak ill of his master it is only as a private individual, and it is not in his power to bring to his notice what he has said (which is the only balm in vengeance). Neither can he convince himself that what has been said about him has not been heard, because he knows with what delight the words of those in authority are received daily.

143

Wherefore I counsel you very seriously, my son, never to permit yourself any freedom in this matter, and to consider that affronts of this kind wound not only those who receive them, but also very often offend those who feign to hear them with the greateſt applause, because when they see us holding in contempt those serving us juſt as they themselves, they fear with good reason that we may treat them in the same way on another occasion.

For, in short, you should take this as the foundation of everything, that to those occupying our rank nothing is pardoned. On the contrary, it often happens that quite indifferent remarks uttered by us without any design are applied by those who hear them either to themselves or to others of whom often enough we are not thinking. And although in reality we are not obliged to have particular regard to every impertinent conjeſture, this should, however, compel us to be more cautious over our words in general in order at leaſt to avoid giving any reasonable foundation to thoughts which might be formed to the prejudice of our service.

On the Italian side I had not at that time any affairs of great importance. A difficulty had arisen at the Court of Savoy over the attitude which the new Duchess [98] should observe towards my Ambassador, because she claimed to aſt in the same manner as the late Duchess, my Aunt. But I made her husband, the Duke, consider that although that Princess, as his wife, bore the same title in his States as his mother, she muſt not claim to be considered in the same way by the reſt of the world ; that the quality of Fille de France from all time had given quite unique prerogatives, and that Princesses formerly honoured with them (whoever the Prince they married) always retained from the head of their family the title and rank of Queen. So the honours rendered to them should not be considered of too much importance. These reasons seemed so good to the Duke of Savoy that he did not feel justified in maintaining his claim any longer.

The Pope and the Duchess of Mantua had a dispute over which they had agreed to recognise me as arbiter. But the matter adjusted itself.

The Duc de Chaulnes, whom I had sent as Ambassador Extraordinary to Rome, had been received there with great honour, for the bad state of health of the Pope at that time was making his nephews a little more polite than had been their custom.99 As soon, however, as the Pope had regained his health they resumed their usual arrogance.

The only question remaining to me to discuss at that Court was to put an end to the divisions which had formed among the clergy of this realm over the propositions of Jansenius. The Pope at first had given very keen attention to the question, as being one which in reality concerned his interests more than mine, and had rendered himself solicitous towards me as regards the carrying out of the provisions of the Bulls he had promulgated on the matter, principally in connection with the Bishops who had refused to obey them.100 I, for my part, readily afforded him the assistance of my authority, but with all due precautions, nevertheless, so as not to prejudice the ancient privileges of the Gallican Church.

Afterwards, however, when I was working on this plan in good faith and had brought matters to a point where the Pope had nothing more to do than nominate the Commissioners, I perceived a change in his behaviour. The reason of this change was that his nephews had interpreted the Christian zeal with which I was acting in the matter as proceeding from active political jealousy, and imagined that they could extract from me anything they pleased, in return for the satisfaction they would give me on this head.

So when my Ambassador spoke to them on my behalf about the nominating of the Commissioners they first of all made various difficulties, and then, explaining themselves more precisely, dared to propose that, in exchange for this, I should consent to pull down the pyramid which they had been constrained to build for me in reparation for the crime of the Corsicans.[101]   But at this, in order to show that I had no other desire in the matter than the good of religion, and that in what concerned the interests of my State I did not fear Jansenism at all, I ordered my Ambassador to tell these gentlemen simply, that after having informed His Holiness of the state of affairs, and having laid before him what had to be done, according to due form, in the execution of his own decrees, I felt that I had fulfilled my duty towards God, and that it would rest with His Holiness for the future to do his when it should please him.

Meanwhile, Cardinal Orsini, whose behaviour (as you have seen in the past years) had not been what it should,[102] presented himself at my Court and, having given evidence of real repentance for his fault, I decided to forget it, and to restore to him the title of Comprotecteur de France which I had taken from him.

Soon afterwards I re-established discipline and union in the Order of Cîteaux. Division had been caused by the machinations or ill-considered zeal of certain individual Superiors who, under the pretext of a more austere reconstitution, desired to remove themselves from the authority of the General, who, for his part, maintained that the new regulations to which the reformers wished to conform could not absolve them from the obedience they owed to their natural Superior.

This matter appeared to me to be the more worthy of my attention as the Order was extremely celebrated, and the schism thereby disclosed was giving general scandal to the whole Church, in addition to the fact that as it had been begun in the year 1633, by Cardinal de La Rochefoucauld, a man of ability and singular piety, and had since been followed up, not only in all the provinces of the kingdom, but even before the Pope himself, it had not been possible to put an end to it.

So I had the matter brought before my Council, but (as if it had been fated that this affair should never be ended) the members of my Council were divided in their opinion, and I found myself under the necessity of deciding it by my vote alone, which I gave in favour of the General. For beyond the fundamental reasons which it would be tedious to enumerate here, and the sentiments of the Pope who had judged the question as I had, I considered that it was to the advantage of the State to keep all the monasteries abroad who offered to range themselves on his side, under the obedience of the Head of the Order, and that it was prudent in a sovereign to support those vested with the character of Superior against the revolt of subordinates in all things that were just.

I further proposed at that time another regulation which concerned the State as well as the Church. This was in regard to the Feasts, the number of which, supplemented from time to time by special devotions, appeared to me to be harmful to individual welfare by keeping people away too often from their work, so that it diminished the prosperity of the kingdom by lessening the amount of the output of manufactures, and that it was prejudicial even to the religion by which it was enjoined because the majority of the artisans were coarse fellows, and, as a rule, gave up these precious days, which were destined solely for prayer and good works, to debauchery and disorder.

With this in my mind I thought that it would be for the good of the people and of God's service to introduce some moderation in these matters, and brought my views to the notice of the Archbishop of Paris, who judged them to be full of reason, and as the Pastor of the capital of my kingdom, was quite willing to give an example in this matter to all his brethren.

The impieties which were being committed in the Vivarais gave occasion to my causing to be held in that district Special Sessions of the officials of the Parliament of Toulouse, and although the correlated chamber of Castres begged me urgently to allow a place in that tribunal for some of their deputies, as having the right to take part therein, I thought it would be more in the interests of religion not to grant them this request, which I contrived to evade by divers delays while the affair was being concluded.

A like zeal caused me to send the Abbé de Bourséis to Portugal to endeavour to convert Schomberg [103] who had acquired a considerable reputation there, and to try and obtain reparation from the Dutch for the scandal they had caused shortly before in regard to a chaplain belonging to my Ambassador.

Soon afterwards I dismissed the Assembly which had been sitting since the beginning of June, and assessed the special donation, which it was customary for them to make me every five years, in the sum of eight hundred thousand *écus*, although up till then it had refrained from doing so either on account of the desire of the deputies to continue their stay in Paris, or from the wish to spare their purses.

I have never failed, when an occasion has presented itself, to impress upon you the great respect we should have for religion, and the deference we should show to its ministers in matters specially connected with their mission, that is to say, with the celebration of the Sacred Mysteries and the preaching of the doctrine of the Gospels. But because people connected with the Church are liable to presume a little too much on the advantages attaching to their profession, and are willing sometimes to make use of them in order to whittle down their most rightful duties, I feel obliged to explain to you certain points on this question which may be of importance.

The first is that Kings are absolute *seigneurs*, and from their nature have full and free disposal of all property both secular and ecclesiastical, to use it as wise dispensers, that is to say, in accordance with the requirements of their State.

The second is that those mysterious names, the Franchises and Liberties of the Church, with which perhaps people will endeavour to dazzle you, have equal reference to all the faithful whether they be laymen or tonsured, who are all equally sons of this common Mother ; but that they exempt neither the one nor the other from subjection to Sovereigns, to whom the Gospel itself precisely enjoins that they should submit themselves.

The third is that all that people say in regard to any particular destination of the property of the Church, and to the intention of founders, is a mere scruple without foundation, because it is certain that, inasmuch as the founders of benefices when transmitting their succession were not able to free them either from the quit-rental or the other dues which they paid to particular *seigneurs*, so for a far stronger reason they could not release them from the first due of all which is payable to the Prince as *Seigneur* over all, for the general welfare of the whole realm.

The fourth is that if up till now permission has been given to ecclesiastics to deliberate in their assemblies on the amount which it is their duty to provide, they should not attribute this custom to any special privilege, because the same liberty is still left to the people of several provinces as a former mark of the probity existing in the first centuries, when justice was sufficient to animate each individual to do what he should according to his ability and, notwithstanding, this never prevented either laymen or ecclesiastics when they refused to fulfil their obligations of their own free will, from being compelled to do so.

And the fifth and last is that if there are dwellers in our Empire more bound than others to be of service to us as regards their property as a whole, these should be the beneficiaries who only hold all they have at our option. The claims attaching to them have been established as long as those of their benefices, and we have titles to them which have been preserved from the first period of the monarchy. Even Popes who have striven to despoil us of this right have made it more clear and more incontestable by the precise retractation of their ambitious pretensions which they have been obliged to make.

But we might say that in this matter there is no need of either titles or examples, because natural equity alone is sufficient to illustrate this point. Would it be just that the Nobility should give its services and its blood in the defence of the realm and so often consume its resources in the maintenance of the offices with which it is charged, and that the people (with so little substance and so many mouths to fill) should bear in addition the sole weight of all the expenses of the State, while ecclesiastics, exempt by their profession from the dangers of war, from the profusion of luxury and the burden of families, should enjoy in abundance all the advantages of the general public without ever contributing anything to its necessities ?

In the midst of all my other labours, what was most in my mind was to place myself in a position to get back from the hands of the King of Spain the provinces which fell to my lot at the death of the King, his Father.[104] And, inasmuch as nothing was more important for this purpose than to make an end of the other affairs in which I was engaged on behalf of the Dutch in order to be free to use all my resources in my own quarrel, I first arranged a conference in Germany between the States and the Bishop of Munster, at which Colbert, *maître des requêtes*, attended to represent me, and soon brought matters to a conclusion.[105] And I then endeavoured to utilise the good intentions of the Queen of England in order to make peace with her son, the King.[106]

The first advantage I obtained from the intervention of the Queen of England was to settle an incidental dispute which was raised by the King. For he claimed, not without some reason, that the Treaty ought to be made by him, because the Dutch, who were the real party with whom he had to treat, were his inferiors in point of dignity. Nevertheless, after some disputing, he relinquished this claim on my remonstrating that the House of the Queen, his Mother, might be accepted by us as neutral ground, and that it was fitting to the dignity of that Princess that the peace, after having been proposed by her, should be negotiated in her presence, and with her participation. But what made me support this suggestion the more readily was that I saw that from the very respect due to the presence of the Queen means would be found to curtail most of the preliminary questions which, as a rule, lengthen out treaties ; besides, as matters would be negotiated so close to me, I should have facility to inspire continually my ministers with what would be to my interest. Our representatives, accordingly, assembled at the spot agreed upon. But my Lord Holles, who was treating for the King of England, having represented at the first conference that he could listen to no proposition if it were not first agreed to yield to his master the King all the clauses which he had proposed some time before through the intermediary of the Portuguese Ambassador, matters advanced no further. And this *milord* was recalled soon after by his master the King.

This did not, however, cause our mediatrix to despair of succeeding in what she had undertaken. Promising herself that Holles or some other representative would soon come from England, she begged me that if he should return during a voyage to Bourbon which she was desirous of making for her health, the conferences should continue at her house under the same forms as if she had been present.

Holles, however, did not come back, and, to tell the truth, I was not greatly distressed over this, for during the stay he had made at my Court as Ambassador, I had noticed in him a bluntness of mind ill-suited to negotiate an agreement, and I do not even know for what purpose he had feigned excuses for remaining here after the war had terminated his mission, up till the time when he was entrusted to treat of the peace. But we were not long in renewing fresh negotiations through the relations maintained by Ruvigny with the Comte de Saint-Alban, who was then in England, and who gave us hope from day to day that he would return with reasonable proposals. What was moſt inconvenient to me about these *pourparlers* was that while I was as impatient to advance the matter as I possibly could be, I was unable, nevertheless, to hurry it on without doing myself considerable harm. For on the side of the English this would have made them demand most unjuſt conditions, and on that of the Dutch, it would have created jealousies which would put back the affair inſtead of advance it, because there was nothing in the world they feared so ſtrongly as to see me eſtablished in their neighbourhood.

I endeavoured, nevertheless, on every occasion to reassure their minds on this point ; and one day, in a conversation with Van Beuningen,[107] I made him underſtand (in general terms) that too much diſtrust between allies often caused much harm to both parties. Whereupon, on his replying that he saw nothing which could cause diſtruſt to the States except the encroachment upon Flanders which I seemed desirous of making, I showed him that although my rights in the Low Countries extended over certain provinces which were near to them, I should always be ready to transfer them to other territories for a consideration. But I only mentioned this to him, however, as a queſtion which could be discussed at leisure, in order that my diligence might anticipate whatever decision the States took in the matter.

With this in view I always made the pretext of the war on the sea cover all the preparations I was making. I required large ſtores of provisions on the side of Flanders, but I colleſted them in my maritime ports as though for the purpose of providing at need all the requirements of my ships ; and I also gave orders that they should supply the Dutch from them with all that they might ask. There was in reality a large quantity of flour in the other ſtrong places, but these ſtores were accounted for by the fresh concern I had taken that year to provision my troops myself, and out of this arrangement I also made a specious pretext to keep the larger portion of them in Picardy and Champagne, so that in these two provinces alone I had at leaſt fifty thousand men ready to enter Flanders at the firſt orders.

I gave out meantime, to provide people something to talk about, that I was going to make a journey to Breſt, and often counted the days when speaking to my servants, and even drew up the orders which were to be observed during the march of my household troops.

As regards the Spaniards, I entertained them with the proposal of a new commercial Treaty. And knowing that an offensive and defensive league between them and the English was under discussion, in order to cause delay I conceived the idea of offering the Catholic King to make a similar one with him, and even to include the King of Portugal, which it was not possible for the English to do. Over this proposal the Spaniards were sufficiently simple-minded to delay a fairly long time.

Meantime, I passed over various things to which I could have drawn attention in other circumſtances. For all the time reports were coming to me that Caſtel Rodrigo, the Governor of the Low Countries, was causing or permitting outrages on all the French who were there, and was giving them no juſtice. At this I expressed no resentment, but was not vexed when certain Spanish couriers, who were passing through on their way to Flanders, were robbed.

In the same manner I said nothing about the proteⅽtion which was being given at Madrid to Saint-Aunay,[108] one of my subjects who was showing himself very insolent towards me ; and it was without my wish or participation that the Comte de la Feuillade went there and compelled that man to write him a letter disavowing the authorship of a skit which had been imputed to him.

Meanwhile, I did not neglect to have accurate plans drawn up of all the fortified places in Flanders, and especially of Bouchain, at which place I then had in mind to make a beginning.

But what I found held most difficulty in all my labours to forward this enterprise was to make sure of the Swedes who, owing to the minority of their Prince, were being governed by a kind of Senate, all of whose decisions were influenced by the interests of the present. They had already made this sufficiently clear by their proceedings in regard to me and the King of England, for when that Prince made overtures to them to league himself with him against the King of Denmark, their former enemy, they first gave him their word to do so, and afterwards, notwithstanding, retracted it out of consideration for me.

This, however, was not brought about without difficulty. At the first remonstrances I made to them they were careful for some time to offer me a general undertaking not to engage themselves on any side against me ; and again afterwards, when I informed them that I was aware of the formal understanding they had with the King of Great Britain to go to war with the King of Denmark, and that at this juncture to declare war against that Prince (Denmark) was to declare war against me, they told me that it had never been in their minds to take sides against France, and that if they were favourably disposed towards the King of England as against the Dutch, it was because they had believed I should range

myself on the same side in view of the near relationship I bore to that Prince.

But while I was considering various means to make
them alter this decision, their eagerness to follow their
own interests caused them to come round of their own
accord to everything I could wish. For at that time I
owed them one hundred thousand *écus*, the arrears
of old standing monies which I had put off paying on
purpose ; and in addition they hoped to obtain from
me fresh assistance in money for their enterprise in
Bremen.[109] And this decided them to send me Koenigsmark as Ambassador Extraordinary,[110] with orders to offer
their mediation between me and the King of England,
which undoubtedly meant an engagement to remain
neutral. But there still remained some element of
deception in these overtures, because their mediation
was only offered to me and to the States of Holland,
without any mention of the King of Denmark, concerning
whom I was desirous that they should explain themselves.
As the Ambassador endeavoured to make me pass over
this omission as a matter that they had not considered
at all, and one on which he had no instructions to give
me an answer, I obliged him to send to Sweden to obtain
a decision. Meanwhile, for my part, I delayed giving
any reply to his requests. The answer came soon afterwards in conformity with my intentions, in such wise
that the King of Denmark was entirely relieved of fear
from the Swedes. I then handed over to them the
hundred thousand *écus* of the old debt.

But as regards the fresh demand they made on me, I
replied to the Ambassador that if they were willing to
conclude the Treaty he was negotiating between us I
would willingly consent to a sum in ready money being
included in it to meet their needs ; that the matter had

not been subjected to any delay up till then on my part, nor would be now, and that it only rested with them to put an end to it.

However, some little time after, fearing that this refusal might anger them, and being unwilling to grudge a moderate sum to gain them over if possible, I decided to give them a further hundred thousand *écus*. But I did not wish to aprise them of this through the channel of Koenigsmark, although he was pressing me keenly on this subject, because I thought that Arnauld, who was acting for me in Sweden and would have to be my spokesman, would obtain a greater advantage for my affairs, which otherwise seemed to be in a fairly favourable condition.

For I received nothing but obliging language from the Swedes. Queen Christine III had asked my good offices with them in what regarded her own interests, and out of consideration to me they had promised to treat her in the most honourable manner possible, and even in the matter of our Treaty they had already declared positively that they were very willing to enter into a league with me against the House of Austria. We had already communicated to each other the articles we proposed to insert, and I, for my part, had even given replies to the demands of the Swedes.

There also occurred at this time an event which was well calculated to forward these negotiations. This was the settlement of Bremen. As their troops, for this reason, were no longer required, it seemed that they must be very glad to have an opportunity of putting them to some use.

In fact, whether they were influenced by this consideration, and on that account had a mind to do what I wished, or whether they only intended to put me at loggerheads with the House of Austria in order to make all they could out of it afterwards at their leisure, they gave me greater hopes than ever, and making a serious effort to reconcile me with the King of England they pressed him to accept their mediation. He declined this at first under various pretexts. But the only reason which really affected him was his repugnance to accept as arbitrators people who were definitely engaged to follow his side.

This does not mean that the Swedes did not bring forward many excuses for their want of good faith, saying among other things, that they were threatened by immediate war on the part of the Muscovites, and that it was not reasonable that they should bind themselves to support the quarrel of their allies to the prejudice of their own security. But it was easy to discern that the real reason of their behaviour was solely because they looked to obtain greater advantage in leaving the King of England on this occasion than in helping him as they had promised.

From this I think you should learn two things : one, that neither the sanctity of treaties, nor the good faith of promises once given are strong enough to hold back those who by nature are untrustworthy ; and the other, that for the execution of our plans we must base them only on our knowledge of our own capabilities. Although it is incumbent on the probity of a Prince to keep his word under all circumstances, it is not prudent in him to trust that of others absolutely.

We should also realise that in this matter the strongest precautions are useless. There is no clause so clearly defined that it does not encounter varied interpretations, and the moment one has taken the resolution to go back upon it, a pretext can easily be found. In treaties every one uses words to suit present interests, but the majority endeavour afterwards to explain their words according to the circumstances as they arrive, and when the reason which made them give their undertaking no longer exists, few people are found to make their promises hold good.

But I think I should also observe to you here for your particular instruction that this manner of acting is more to be feared from States which are ruled by the suffrages of many than from those at the bidding of one alone. Princes, whose illustrious birth and the uprightness of their education produce as a rule only noble and generous feelings, are unable to let these good principles become corrupted to such a degree that there does not always remain on their minds some impress from them. This conception of virtue, however much obliterated it may become by the corruption of the times, does, nevertheless, always give to the most evil men some kind of repugnance for vice. Their hearts, formed at an early age on the laws of honour, create so strong a habit that they find it hard to corrupt it entirely, and the desire for glory which animates them causes them in many things to rise above the cravings of their interests.

But it is not so with these people of mediocre condition by whom aristocratic States are governed. The decisions of their Councils are not based on any other principle than that of utility. These bodies, formed of such a quantity of heads, do not possess a heart which is capable of being warmed by the fire of generous passions. The joy springing from upright actions, the shame which follows on baseness, gratitude for benefits received, and remembrance of services rendered, when divided among so many persons, end by becoming weakened to such a point that they no longer have any effect, and it is only self-interest alone (as regards individuals as well as the State in general) which has power to give any rule to their conduct.

The instruction which you can draw from these truths, my son, is not that one ought to keep away absolutely from any kind of relationship with States like these. For, on the contrary, I hold that a capable Prince should know how to utilise everything to arrive at his ends. But in our dealings with them this only is necessary, that we must lay down as our principal maxim that whatever we may do in their regard, whether to vex or to oblige them, they will never fail to seek our aid every time they think they see some profit in it, and will also never hesitate to leave us the moment they discover some danger in following us.

As regards the King of England, I could not take a better course to oblige him to make peace with me than by placing myself in a condition to wage a vigorous war against him. With this in view, I formed a plan to take from him the Isle of Jersey, which would be very convenient to me on account of its nearness to Brittany, and would be of infinite service for the purpose of interrupting the trade of the English, which was a matter of special importance ; and there was no doubt that the moment these islanders should find themselves inconvenienced in their commerce, they would straightway compel their King to come to an agreement.

It was with this in view that I also summoned the Dutch to contribute with me in the formation of a powerful squadron during the autumn, with which I hoped to surprise twenty English frigates commissioned as escort to the merchantmen of Tangiers.[112] But the States not being agreed among themselves about it, caused me to lose this opportunity.

Meanwhile, I had new ships built and cannon cast in different places both within and outside my kingdom. I had my depots repeatedly stocked with everything necessary for the navy, and to secure that my fleet should be ready the sooner to put to sea in the next campaign I made the troops who manned it winter on the spot, and, contrary to the usual practice, ordered the naval officers and able seamen to be kept there also.

Elsewhere I was maintaining relations with the Catholics in Ireland, and had already destined troops to go there on the appearance of any rising in that island. I had also some correspondence with a remnant of the Cromwell faction, from whom I received various propositions, among others from Sidney, an English gentleman, who promised me to stir up important risings ; but his proposal that I should advance a hundred thousand *écus* made me distrustful of his promises, and, being unwilling to risk so large a sum on the faith of a fugitive, I only offered him twenty thousand *écus* down, with an undertaking to furnish his adherents with the rest immediately they appeared in a condition to be of service to me.

I daily endeavoured to augment my credit in Germany. Notwithstanding the warfare which I had carried on against the Bishop of Munster, I had always acted very straightforwardly with him as being a man who was capable of various designs, and I placed myself in such good relations with him that immediately he had made peace with the States of Holland he sent to me with an offer of his troops. For my part, I had some difficulty in deciding how I should reply to his overtures. On the one hand, I saw that by accepting them they would not only swell my forces but would diminish those of my enemies as well, to whom undoubtedly they would go over if I refused ; on the other, I reflected that I was still burdened at the time with my naval force which was running into very great expenditure and (what struck me more forcibly) it seemed to me that this would amount to declaring my designs openly, and awakening the suspicions of all who were anxious to oppose them.

I proposed a Treaty with all the Rhine Princes under which all should undertake to join forces in preventing the Emperor from throwing any troops into the Low Countries, while I promised on my part not to send an army into Germany. Count Guillaume de Furstemberg had already made them agree as to the number of men each should arm for this purpose amounting in all to two millions, for whom I sent only four hundred thousand pounds that year to make a beginning of the levies, while waiting for matters to advance elsewhere.

Meanwhile, having been informed that the quarrel that had arisen between the Elector of Mayence and the Palatine over the right of *vilfranc*, of which I think I have already spoken to you, was becoming more heated day by day, in such wise that it was capable of using up the resources of these two Princes, I sent Courtin to them, one of the *maîtres des requêtes* on my establishment, to restore a good understanding between them.

The Marquis of Brandenburg seemed at that time fairly disposed to join with me, as he had himself explained to one of my ministers, because he was claiming to take back the Duchy of Gueldre, over which he had some rights.[113]

A Theatine had been residing for some time at my Court who, although acknowledged by the Electress of Bavaria only, had nevertheless gradually opened some kind of intercourse between me and that Duke from whom shortly after I received various proposals.

Finally, I had further various agents in Hungary in order to give rise to trouble for the Emperor in case he had a mind to mix himself in my affairs. With a view to maintain some connection between all those who were acting for me in the different Courts, I sent Milet to the camp at Bremen who, while keeping observation upon what was going on there, was also informed of what was being done in the neighbouring States, and had orders to report to each of my agents anything that might contribute to my service.

But, although I was working in this manner in foreign countries so as to engage them as far as possible in my interests, I applied myself principally, however, to increasing my own resources, as being the surest means to contribute to the success of my plans.

For a long time I had taken pains to train my household troops, and it was from this corps that I drew nearly all the officers of the new companies which I was raising, in order that they might bring to them the same discipline to which they were accustomed ; and I filled the vacancies with other cavaliers selected from the old regiments, or with young gentlemen, who could not have a better school of instruction.

Meanwhile, I held reviews very often, both of the newly raised troops, to see if they were up to full strength, and also of the old, to find out whether they had been weakened by the new levies, for I instructed the Captains to whom I gave my commissions to pay special attention to enrolling all fresh soldiers presenting themselves, because otherwise it would mean increasing the companies and the expense of their upkeep without augmenting the number of trained soldiers.

With a view to providing more security against this confusion and to ensure that my troops should always remain at full strength, I gave orders for the rosters of the *montres* of all the regiments in my pay to be forwarded to me each month, however far apart they might be ; [114] and in order to learn whether I was being faithfully served in this matter I purposely sent gentlemen to all parts to take the troops by surprise and take note of them unexpectedly, which kept both the Captains and the Commissaries under the continuous obligation of doing their duty.

Then, in order that no one any longer should find excuses for their soldiers deserting—a matter in truth very ruinous for the troops—I decided to apply more effective remedies than those which had served up till then ; and after taking the advice of the men most qualified in military knowledge, I·issued an order, the good results of which have been subsequently recognised.

I was anxious also to remove all matters in dispute which had so often caused disorder among our troops ; and expressing no amazement at all these different claims which each corps urged with so much heat that no one had yet dared to decide them, I regulated all their ranks with as much justice as I could, and upheld my ruling by my authority so well that no one dared contradict it.

In order to equalise, as regards everything, the work and honour due to their service in all infantry regiments, I decided that if the war on the sea continued every one should serve his turn on board ship ; and to increase the affection which the sailors showed for my service I decided in their favour a dispute they had with their captains over their pay which up till then had not always been faithfully given to them.

I curtailed, on my part, the greater portion of my usual expenditure on my pleasure, placing first my principal satisfaction to keep my people contented.

I was unable to prevent myself from increasing on different occasions the companies of my *gardes-de-corps*, because of the large number of people of quality or of

good service who were continually importuning me
for a position in them. But finally I fixed the number
at eight hundred, all of them old soldiers or discharged
officers, with the exception of twenty young gentlemen
whom I apportioned among the companies to learn their
duties.

The eagerness to serve me was so great that the greatest
difficulty I encountered on every occasion which presented
itself was to restrain those who came forward, as happened
when I wished to man my ships at Dieppe. For, over
and above the men who had received orders, such a large
number of volunteers offered themselves that I was
obliged to refuse them all, and even to punish a few of
the highest rank who, with the knowledge that they would
be refused, started off without asking my leave.

I maintained such correct discipline among my troops
that after sending some of them at different times to my
allies in Italy, Hungary, and Holland, they never gave
the least cause for complaint, although sometimes they
had very good reasons to be discontented. I took care
also everywhere to have them paid punctually by a treasurer whom I kept on the strength, and I increased their
ordinary pay in Holland because I was aware that victuals
were dearer there than elsewhere.

On every occasion when I assembled troops within my
kingdom, I was careful to dispatch Commissaries who
made provision on the spot of all things necessary for
their subsistence at the price at which they had been
accustomed to buy for themselves, and sold them afterwards to the soldiers at a rate proportioned to their pay,
in order that they might always have the means to live
without being chargeable on the peasants.

I had so much concern on this point that when going
to Picardy in the month of March to hold a great review,

I would not stay at Compiègne, which was the nearest place, and the most convenient for me and my establishment, because it was a town which was able to house a large part of my infantry who, failing this, would have found billets in the villages where it would have been more difficult to make them live in a disciplined manner.

Inasmuch as the *ustensile* [115] was one of the principal causes of quarrels between their hosts and the soldiers, it was one of the things I took further pains to regulate, fixing the amount for the infantry at a *sol*, and that for the cavalry at three *sols*, of which one-third only was paid by the host, another by the Town Council, and the last by the general who had been chosen. In cases where some contravention or dispute occurred in the execution of my regulations, I gave orders to the Commissaries and Intendants to decide them between the occupier and the soldier without showing any preference. I myself, having learnt that a captain in Auvergne had taken three hundred pounds from the inhabitants of Rethel to exempt them from having troops quartered on them, broke that officer and would not listen to a thousand persons of quality who importuned me on his behalf.

This does not imply that I was not well aware that among people of humble condition from whom spring the soldiers and sometimes non-commissioned officers, the spirit of licentiousness is generally one of the principal motives which make men follow the military profession, and that not long ago there were commanders who over a long period maintained large armies with no other pay than liberty to pillage everywhere. But this example should only be imitated by men who have nothing to lose and have therefore nothing to preserve. For every Prince who cherishes his reputation with any feeling of decency cannot doubt that it is just as incumbent on him to protect the property of his subjects from being pillaged by his own troops as by those of his enemies. And he who gives heed to his affairs will not fail to perceive that all that he suffers to be taken from his people, in what manner soever this may happen, is never taken except at his own cost, because it is manifest that the more his provinces become exhausted, whether at the hands of soldiers or from any other cause, the less are they able to contribute to all the rest of the public charges. It is a great mistake for sovereigns to appropriate to themselves certain things and certain persons as if they belonged to them in any different way from the rest of what they hold under their empire.

The money in their privy purse, what is held in the hands of their treasurers, and what they leave in the commerce of their people, should all alike be managed carefully by them. The troops who are maintained in their own name are not for that reason more their own than those over whom they appoint individual commanders, and those who follow the profession of arms are not more bounden nor more useful in their service than the rest of their subjects.

Each profession in its own way contributes to the maintenance of the monarchy. The labourer provides by his labour food for all this great body ; the artisan by his industry supplies all things serviceable to the convenience of the public, and the merchant collects from a thousand different places everything useful or pleasing produced by the entire world, in order to furnish it to every individual the moment he requires it ; the financiers provide for the subsistence of the State by collecting the public monies ; the judges, by applying

the laws, maintain security among men ; and the ecclesiastics, by instructing the people in religion, draw down
the blessing of Heaven and preserve peace on earth.

For this reason, far from treating with contempt any
of these callings, or favouring one at the expense of the
others, we should be the common father of all of them,
taking pains to bring them, if possible, to as great a degree
of perfection as is suited to each, and we should hold the
firm conviction that even the one to whom we might be
disposed to show an unjust preference will feel no added
affection or esteem for us, while the others will rightly
complain and murmur.

If, however, notwithstanding all these reasons, you are
unable to prevent yourself, my son, from cherishing
that secret predilection which is nearly always held by
generous souls for the profession of arms, take special
care that this personal attraction never leads you to tolerate
the excesses of those who follow it, and so act that your
affection towards them may be seen in the care you
exercise for their proper maintenance and welfare, rather
than in allowing their morals to become corrupted.

REFLECTIONS ON THE *ROLE* OF KING [116]
1679

KINGS ARE OFTEN OBLIGED TO ACT contrary
to their inclination in a way that wounds
their own natural good inftincts. They should
like to give pleasure, and they often have to punish
and ruin people to whom they are naturally well disposed.
The interefts of the State muft come firft. One has to
do violence to one's inclinations, and not place oneself
in the position of having to reproach oneself as regards
any important matter which might have been done better
had not certain private interefts prevented it and turned
aside the views one ought to have in the interefts of
the greatness, the welfare, and the power of the State.

There are often occasions which give trouble ; some
are delicate and difficult to disentangle ; one's ideas
are sometimes confused. So long as that is the case we
can remain without coming to a decision ; but the moment we have settled our mind upon anything, and think
we have seen the beft course, we muft take it ; that
is what has often made me succeed in what I have done.
The miftakes I have made, and which have caused me
infinite trouble, have been caused by kindness, and by
allowing myself to surrender too heedlessly to the advice
of others.

Nothing is so dangerous as weakness, of whatever kind
it be. To command others, one muft raise oneself above

them ; and after having heard all sides one muſt decide on the judgment one may come to with an open mind, always keeping in view to order or do nothing unworthy of oneself, of the charaċter one bears, or of the greatness of the State.

Princes who have good intentions and some knowledge of their affairs from experience or ſtudy, and great application in rendering themselves capable, find so many different channels for making themselves acquainted with them that they should exercise care over the individual and a general solicitude for all.

It is necessary to guard againſt oneself to beware of one's own inclinations, and to be always on the watch over one's natural self. The *rôle* of King is a great one, noble and pleasing when one feels oneself to be worthy of acquitting oneself well in all things undertaken ; but it is not exempt from troubles, fatigue, and anxieties. Uncertainty sometimes makes one lose heart, and when one has spent a reasonable amount of time in examining into a matter one muſt come to a decision, and take the course one believes to be the beſt.

When one has the State in view, one is working for oneself. The good of the one makes the glory of the other. When the State is happy, eminent, and powerful, he who is the cause thereof is covered with glory, and as a consequence has a right to enjoy all that is moſt agreeable in life in a greater degree than his subjeċts, in proportion to his position and theirs.

When one has made a miſtake one muſt repair it as soon as possible, and no consideration, not even goodness of heart, muſt ſtand in the way.

In 1671, a miniſter died who held a poſt of Secretary of State, the Department of Foreign Affairs.[117]   He was a capable man, but one not without his faults ; he did not neglect to fill this post well, which is a very important one. I was some time considering to whom I should hand over his charge and, after having examined into the matter carefully, it seemed good to me that a man who had been serving for long in the Embassies was the one to fill it best.[118] I sent for him ; my choice was approved by every one, a thing that does not always happen. On his return I placed him in possession of his charge. I only knew him by reputation and through commissions with which I had entrusted him, which he had executed well. But the work I had given him was too great and too extended for him. For several years I suffered from his weakness, his obstinacy, and his want of close attention. These cost me a good deal, and I did not profit by all the advantages I might have had—and all this was due to my kindness and good nature. Finally it was necessary for me to order him to resign because all that passed through his hands lost some of the greatness and authority which a man should possess when executing the orders of a King of France, who was no fool. If I had decided to remove him sooner I should have avoided the inconveniences which have happened to me, and I should not be reproaching myself that my kindness to him had done harm to the State. I have mentioned this particular incident as an example of what I have said above.

INSTRUCTIONS TO THE DUC D'ANJOU [119]
1700

1. Never omit any of your duties, especially towards God.

2. Preserve yourself in the purity of your bringing up.

3. Cause God to be honoured in all places where you have power ; procure His glory ; give the example. It is one of the greateſt forms of good that Kings can do.

4. On every occasion declare yourself on the side of virtue and againſt vice.

5. Have no attachment ever to any one.[120]

6. Love your wife, lead a good life with her, and ask God to give you one suitable to you. I do not think you should take an Auſtrian woman.

7. Love the Spaniards and all your subjeĉts attached to your Crowns and to your person ; do not give preference to those who flatter you moſt ; eſteem those who for a good cause venture to displease you ; these are your real friends.

8. Make your subjeĉts happy ; and, with a view to this, only engage in war when you are obliged, and after you have well considered and weighed the reasons with your Council.

9. Endeavour to keep your finances in good order ; watch over the Indies and your fleets ; keep your commerce in mind ; live in close union with France, since

there is nothing so advantageous to our two Powers as this union which nothing can withstand.

10. If you are compelled to go to war, place yourself at the head of your armies.

11. Take thought to re-establish your troops everywhere, and begin with those in Flanders.

12. Never leave your affairs for your pleasure ; but make for yourself a rule of some kind which will give you occasions of liberty and distraction.

13. Of these there is hardly a more innocent one than the chase and the pleasure of some country house, provided that you do not incur too much expense thereon.

14. Pay great attention to your affairs ; when people discuss them with you listen to them at length at the beginning, without deciding anything.

15. When you have attained to more knowledge, remember that it is for you to decide ; but whatever be your experience, always hearken to all the advice and all the arguments of your Council before coming to this decision.

16. Do all in your power to get to know well the most important people, in order that you may make suitable use of them.

17. See that your Viceroys and Governors shall always be Spaniards.

18. Treat every one well ; never say anything vexing to any one, but do honour to people of quality and merit.[121]

19. Give evidence of your gratitude to the late King and to all who sided with choosing you as his successor.

20. Have great confidence in Cardinal Portocarrero, and show him your pleasure in the course he has pursued.

21. I think you should do something considerable for the Ambassador who had the tact to ask for you and to be the first to greet you in the quality of a subject.[122]

22. Do not forget Betmar, who has merit and is capable of being of service to you.

23. Have entire trust in the Duc d'Harcourt ; [123] he is a clever and an honest man, and will only give you advice in accordance with your interests.

24. Keep all Frenchmen in good order.

25. Treat your domestic servants well, but do not allow them too much familiarity, and trust them still less ; use them so long as they are well-behaved ; dismiss them on the least fault they commit and never uphold them against the Spaniards.

26. Have no dealings with the Queen Dowager beyond what you can help ; [124] arrange for her to leave Madrid and not to go out of Spain ; wherever she is keep an eye on her conduct, and prevent her mixing herself up in any affairs ; regard with suspicion those who have too much to do with her.

27. Love your relations always ; [125] keep in mind the grief they have had in leaving you ; keep up a close intercourse with them in great things and small ; ask us for anything you need, or wish to have, which you do not find where you are ; we will do the same with you.

28. Never forget that you are French, and what may happen to you when you have made secure the Spanish succession with children ; visit your kingdoms ; go to Naples and Sicily ; make a stay in Milan, and come to Flanders ; this will be an opportunity of seeing us again ; meanwhile visit Catalonia, Aragon, and the other places ; see what is to be done for Ceuta.

29. Throw some money to the people when you are in Spain, and especially when entering Madrid.

30. Do not appear astonished at the extraordinary figures you will meet ; never make fun of them ; each

country has its peculiar manners and you will soon become accuſtomed to what at firſt will seem moſt surprising to you.

31. Avoid as far as you can granting favours to those who give money to obtain them ; dispense suitably and liberally, and be chary of accepting presents except they be trifling ; if sometimes you cannot help accepting them, give a more valuable one to the donor after allowing a few days to pass.

32. Keep a privy purse in which to put your own money, of which you alone have the key.

33. I will end with one of the moſt important pieces of advice that I can give you : never allow yourself to be ruled ; be the maſter ; have no favourites or prime miniſter ; liſten to, and consult your Council, but do you decide yourself. God, who made you King, will give you the lights which are necessary to you, so long as you have a right intention.

PLAN OF A SPEECH [126]

1710

I HAVE SUSTAINED THIS WAR with the high hand and
pride which becomes this realm ; through the
valour of my Nobility and the zeal of my subjects
I have been successful in the undertakings I have accomplished for the good of the State ; I have given my
whole concern and application to reach a successful issue ;
I have also put in motion the measures I thought necessary
in fulfilling my duties, and in making known the love
and tenderness I have for my people, by procuring
by my labours a peace which will bring them rest for the
remainder of my reign so that I need have no other care
than for their welfare. After having extended the
boundaries of this Empire, and protected my frontiers
with the important strongholds I have taken, I have
given ear to the proposals of peace which have been made
to me, and I have exceeded perhaps on this occasion the
limits of prudence in order to accomplish so great a work.
I may say that I stepped out of my own character and
did extreme violence to myself in order promptly to secure
repose for my subjects at the expense of my reputation,
or at least of my own particular satisfaction, and perhaps
of my renown, which I willingly risked for the advantage
of those who have enabled me to acquire it. I felt
that I owed them this mark of gratitude. But seeing
at this hour [127] that my most vehement enemies have

only wished to play with me and that they have employed all the artifices they could to deceive me as well as their allies by forcing them to contribute to the immense expenditure which their disordered ambition demanded, I do not see any other course to take than that of considering how to protect ourselves securely, making them understand that a France thoroughly united is stronger than all the powers they have got together at so great pains, by force and artifice, to overwhelm her. Up to now [128] I have made use of the extraordinary measures which on similar occasions I have put into practice in order to provide sums proportionate to the expenditure indispensable to uphold the glory and safety of the State. Now that all sources are *quasi*-exhausted I come to you at this juncture to ask your counsel and your assistance, whence a safe issue will arise. Our enemies will learn from the efforts we shall put forth together that we are not in the condition they would have people believe, and by means of the help which I am asking of you and which I believe to be indispensable, we shall be able [129] to force them to make a peace which shall be honourable to ourselves, lasting for our tranquillity, and agreeable to all the Princes of Europe. This is what I shall look to up to the moment of its conclusion, even in the greatest stress of the war, as well as to the welfare and happiness of my people which have always been, and will continue to be to the last moment of my life, my greatest and most serious concern.

NOTES

Page 41. (1) "I have heard him say this to M. de Paris and Hardouin de Péréfixe, the tutor of Louis XIV, and afterwards Archbishop of Paris." (Note by Pellisson in the Grimoard manuscript.)

Page 42. (2) The Treaty of the Pyrénées was signed on 7th December 1659; the marriage of Louis XIV with the Infanta Marie-Thérèse was celebrated at Saint Jean de Luz on 9th June 1660; Mazarin died at the Château de Vincennes on 9th March 1661.

Page 42. (3) Here begins a picture of the interior and exterior position of France, the methodical division of which into articles is found in Colbert's notes previously written in 1663.

Page 43. (4) The Jansenist dispute, which was started in 1653 by the publication of the *Augustinus*, and further aroused by the *Provinciales* (1656–1657), was then very keen. Several Bishops had just refused to sign the formulary drawn up by the Assembly of the Clergy in February 1661 on the five Propositions attributed to Jansenius and condemned by the Pope.

Page 44. (5) Cardinal de Retz, who was then outside France, had joined the side of the Jansenists in order to be able to negotiate his return, which he effected, as a matter of fact, some time after.

Page 45. (6) It is *piquant* to recall that this passage of the Memoirs was written shortly after the presentation of *Les Plaideurs* (Racine).

Page 46. (7) The reign of Philip IV, great-grandson of Charles V, had been disastrous for Spain; Portugal had revolted and become independent; Catalonia and the Kingdom of Naples had been in rebellion for a long time; France, by the Treaty of the Pyrénées, had snatched Le Roussillon and a part of Artois. So much so that the title of Great, assigned in advance to the King by his minister Olivarez, was a matter for jesting among his subjects; they coined an emblem for him with this device : *Plus on lui ôte, plus il est grand.* His son, Charles II, who was to succeed him in 1665, was born in 1661 and was always in precarious health. Don Louis de Haro replaced Olivarez as minister in 1643 and died in 1661

Page 46. (8) Leopold I, elected in 1658 and died in 1705.

Page 46. (9) The manuscript bears in this place a marginal note by Pellisson : "The King improved this passage ; I could not well remember his exact phrases, and I may have omitted other things besides." The context shows that "The King improved this passage" signifies "put into better words." Louis XIV had therefore given by word of mouth a rendering which Pellisson had not remembered accurately—a valuable sidelight on the work of the Memoirs.

Page 46. (10) The *Ligue du Rhin*, which placed some of the German Princes on the side of France, was formed in 1658.

Page 46. (11) Charles Gustave, King of Sweden, died in 1660 after brilliant campaigns. His son, Charles XI, was only fifteen in 1661.

Page 46. (12) Denmark barely escaped. being entirely conquered by Charles Gustave. It was ruled at that time by Frederic III to whom the States had just restored the supreme power. Up to the death of that Prince it enjoyed the tranquillity it required after the rude shock it had undergone.

Page 47. (13) Charles II, son of the unfortunate Charles I, who was beheaded in 1649, had been proclaimed King in 1660. Henrietta of France, his mother, was the sister of Louis XIII.

Page 47. (14) Holland at that time was a rival of England in commerce against whom she concluded a defensive alliance with France. The States General feared the ambition of the House of Orange which held the office of Stadtholder or Commandership-in-Chief of the troops.

Page 47. (15) Fabio Chigi was elected Pope in 1655 and took the name of Alexander VII. Mazarin had opposed his election.

Page 47. (16) Christine of France, the widow of Duke Victor Amédée I and the mother of the reigning Duke Charles Emmanuel II, was the sister of Louis XIII.

Page 47. (17) The Turks at that time were pressing Candia, a Venetian possession, and numerous Frenchman went to her aid.

Page 47. (18) Ferdinand, the Grand Duke of Tuscany. His son, who was to succeed under the name of Cosmo III, married, on 19th April 1661, Marguerite Louise, daughter of Gaston of Orleans.

Page 49. (19) The concluding portion of this sentence from " with the exception of foreign ministers " was added by Pellisson at the request of Louis XIV, who wrote on the manuscript with his own hand : ". . . with the exception of foreign ministers who sometimes find too favourable moments in the familiarity allowed to them, either to obtain or to discover something."

Page 52. (20) Louis XIV received petitions at the public audiences which he held on certain days. We have here a survival of the direct and patriarchal form of the former method of justice, as practised by Saint Louis under the oak tree at Vincennes.

Page 54. (21) At that time La Mothe-Houdancourt was Bishop of Rennes, and Hardouin de Péréfixe Bishop of Rodez.

Page 54. (22) The celebrated Chancellor Séguier. He was seventy-three years old in 1661.

Page 55. (23) These three persons formed the *Conseil Etroit* under the King, to which Foreign Affairs were reserved by Louis XIV.

Page 55. (24) Michel le Tellier, Secretary of State for War and for the Levantine Marine, the father of Louvois.

Page 55. (25) Hughes de Lionne, who replaced Brienne in Foreign Affairs in 1666.

Page 56. (26) Fouquet had been Superintendent of Finance since 1653. Pellisson, who had been his friend, remained faithful to him after his disgrace; it must have cost him something to transcribe this paragraph, which, contrary to his custom, he copied word for word from Périgny's text.

Page 56. (27) Colbert was appointed Controller of the Finances on 8th March 1661.

Page 57. (28) Henri Auguste de Loménie, Comte de Brienne, Secretary of State for Foreign Affairs and for the Western Marine, was then sixty-six years old. His son, Henri Louis, took his place at his death in 1666, but only for a short time.

Page 57. (29) Louis Phelippeaux, Marquis de la Vrillière, Secretary of State for the Affairs of the So-Called Reformed Religion; and Du Plessis Guénégaud, Secretary of State to the King's Household, who gave up his post to Colbert. With the two other Secretaries of State, Le Tellier and Brienne, they united with the Chancellor, Fouquet the Controller, and Lionne, to form the *Conseil des Dépêches*, which attended to current affairs on Mondays and Thursdays.

Page 67. (30) The *Cours des Aides* assessed the amount to be levied on the people to meet the expenses of the State. (Translator's note.)

Page 74. (31) The château Trompette at Bordeaux, and the citadel of Bordeaux had been begun under Mazarin for the purpose of keeping these two towns within bounds when necessary, as they were often inclined to mix themselves up in popular disturbances.

Page 75. (32) Marguerite Louise of Orleans, who married Cosmo III de Médicis.

Page 75. (33) Philippe of Orleans married Henrietta of England as his first wife.

Page 75. (34) Charles II married Catherine of Portugal, the daughter of King John IV, on the 31st May.

Page 76. (35) The Treaty of the Pyrénées provided that France should not intervene in favour of the Portuguese who were fighting for their independence. Turenne advised sending into Portugal Marshal Schomberg, a foreigner, with four thousand French soldiers raised under cover of the name of the King of Portugal.

Page 77. (36) Louis XIV, in his correspondence with his Ambassador at Marrid, complained of the non-execution of twenty-six points contained in the Treaty of the Pyrénées.

Page 78. (37) Edward Hyde, Earl of Clarendon, on account of his psychological temperament, nicknamed "The Chancellor of Human Nature."

Page 78. (38) La Baſtide de la Croix, who had previously been employed in negotiations with Cromwell.

Page 80. (39) Genoa at that time was an ariſtocratic republic. She had given in to France on several occasions during the preceding centuries; thus she was governed in the name of the King of France from 1396 to 1409, from 1458 to 1460, from 1499 to 1522, and in 1527 and 1528.

Page 80. (40) " Since 1528 " (marginal note by Pellisson).

Page 85. (41) Ferdinand Marie, Elector of Bavaria, disclaimed his deputy at the Electoral Diet, who, at the inſtigation of the Electress, had solicited the Imperial Crown on his behalf. " Madame," he declared to his mother, " I would rather be a rich Elector than a poor Emperor."

Page 85. (42) " Amongſt others, there was one in 921, which was a Treaty of Alliance entered into at Bonn on the Rhine, between Charles the Simple and Henri of Saxe, surnamed the Fowler, in which Charles is always named firſt, and even his witnesses before those of Henri V. André Du Chesne, in the second volume of the *Anciens Hiſtoriens Français*, p. 587." (Marginal note by Pellisson.)

Page 86. (43) Charles Gaspar de la Pierre, Archbishop of Trèves from 1652 to 1676, contracted in 1661 a Treaty of Alliance with Louis XIV, and entered the Ligue du Rhin.

Page 86. (44) The *Alliance* or *Ligue du Rhin* had been formed in 1658 on the initiative of the King of France, under colour of maintaining the Treaties of Weſtphalia, and with a view to preventing the Emperor interfering in favour of the Spanish branch of the House of Auſtria. It had already enabled France to sign the Treaty of the Pyrénées in 1659 advantageously to herself. It included originally the Electors of Cologne and Mayence, the Count Palatine, the Dukes of

Brunswick and Luneburg, the Landgrave of Hesse, and the King of Sweden as being Duke of Bremen. It was renewed in 1661 when the Elector of Trèves joined it.

Page 86. (45) This refers to ten towns in Alsace, the protectorate over which, together with Alsace, had been given to France by the Treaty of Munster: Haguenau, Landau, Wissembourg, Rosheim, Obernai, Sélestat, Kaysersberg, Turkheim, Colmar, and Munster.

Page 87. (46) Alexandre Guillaume, Prince d'Epinoy, Marquis de Roubaix and Governor of Tournay, belonged to an old family of Flanders, but he had attached himself to France long before the reunion of that province, and on that account had been deprived of his possessions by the Spaniards on the declaration of the previous war.

Page 87. (47) The Pays d'Alleu, a small canton comprising three parishes and part of a fourth, was situated between Artois, Flanders, and the Barony of Lille. It had been in dispute between Spain and France since the Treaty of the Pyrénées. It was not re-united to the government of Artois until 1717.

Page 87. (48) France had acquired by the Treaty of the Pyrénées the greater part of Artois.

Page 88. (49) A preceding paragraph was suppressed in the revision. It was concerning God, which explains why the compiler did not repeat the word here.

Page 88. (50) In 1661, Louis XIV, encouraged by public opinion, proposed to the Pope, to the Emperor, and to Venice, a league against the Turks.

Page 88. (51) In 1663, Louis XIV, as a member of the Ligue du Rhin, sent in aid of the Emperor 6,000 men instead of the 2,400 due from him—five fine regiments who went to fight the Turks as to a *fête*, and had a large share in the victory of Saint Gothard.

Page 89. (52) The Comtesse de Soissons, Mistress of the Robes, had a difference with the Duchesse de Navailles, Lady-in-Waiting to the Queen, in connection with their duties, and considered herself to have been slighted by the King's arbitration; her husband in consequence provoked the Duc de Navailles, who refused to take up his challenge.

Page 89. (53) The gentlemen of Port Royal and their pupils were dispersed in 1661.

Page 89. (54) The French had taken Dunkerque from the Spaniards in 1658, but they were obliged to hand it over to England as the price of her alliance. In 1662, Louis XIV bought back this city from Charles II for the sum of four millions.

Page 89. (55) We must remember that this was written fifteen years before the Revocation of the Ediĉt of Nantes, the date of which was 1685.

Page 94. (56) This refers, as we know, to Bossuet and Montausier. The manuscript has here, in Pellisson's handwriting : " Pass over from page 148 to page 184, to the words : *" Plusieurs de. . . ."* (Many of my anceŝtors. . . .) We have therefore conformed to this direĉtion, omitting from our text six or eight pages in which the King speaks of the reasons for faith. This passage, with the exception of a few expressions, may be found in Volume I of Grouvelle's edition, pp. 94 to 100.

Page 95. (57) Philip IV of Spain died on 17th September 1665. Louis XIV counted on taking advantage of the faĉt that his wife, the Infanta Marie Thérèse, was the only child of the firŝt marriage of that Prince. He, together with his wife, had plainly renounced by the Treaty of the Pyrénées all rights to the succession of Spain, but he complained that the Spaniards had not fulfilled certain minor clauses of the Treaty, and from this drew an argument againŝt his renunciation.

Page 95. (58) England, jealous of the competition of the trade of Holland, principally on the coaŝts of Guinea, had declared war againŝt her on 4th March 1665. France was bound to Holland by a Treaty of defensive alliance which Louis XIV had concluded in 1662 to secure her support on the Flanders border againŝt the Spaniards.

Page 97. (59) The War of Independence, which the Portuguese were ŝtill carrying on againŝt Spain, was a fortunate diversion on that border for Louis XIV ; he supported it secretly and wished to see it continue. Peace was concluded, after a ŝtruggle laŝting twenty-six years, in 1668, by which the independence of Portugal was assured.

Page 98. (60) A ŝtrong place near Dunkerque. Louis was fearing an attack on it by the English.

Page 99. (61) The Duc de Beaufort was in command of the fleet. Vivonne was made Commander of the smaller ships in 1665, with authority to take the command in Beaufort's absence.

Page 99. (62) The Queen Mother, Henrietta of France, had been living in France since 1644, whither she had retired after the Revolution in England.

Page 100. (63) Alphonse VI married Marie de Savoie, Duchesse de Nemours, on 10th March 1666.

Page 100. (64) The manuscript gives *Romainville* ; it really has reference to the Abbé of Saint Romain, who is named correĉtly elsewhere in the text of the Memoirs a little further on.

Page 100. (65) This refers to the application of one of the clauses of the Ligue du Rhin to which these Princes were parties.

Page 100. (66) Louis XIV wished to uphold the interests, not only of Holland, but also of Poland, an old enemy of Sweden.

Page 101. (67) Szerini, a Hungarian patriot, opposed to the dominion of the Emperor.

Page 101. (68) The Duke of Bavaria desired to be elected King of the Romans. Louis XIV showed some condescension to his designs in order to detach him from the Emperor.

Page 101. (69) The right of *Wildfang* (capture) permitted the Elector Palatine to reduce to a kind of slavery any strangers who settled on his lands or on those of the neighbouring Princes, whence this dispute of the Elector with his neighbours.

Page 102. (70) Charles Colbert de Vendières, Marquis de Croissy, was a younger brother of the great Colbert. He was often employed on delicate diplomatic missions, and in 1679 became Secretary of State for Foreign Affairs. *Maître des Requêtes*, one who held the authority of a Magistrate.

Page 104. (71) Anne of Austria died on 20th January 1666.

Page 106. (72) The Procurators and Attorney-Generals were called *Gens du Roi*.

Page 107. (73) The *Chambres des Enquêtes* formed a section of the Parliament of Paris.

Page 108. (74) The Duc de Valois, only son of Monsieu (younger brother of Louis XIII) and Henrietta of England. He died during the month of December 1666.

Page 109. (75) Gaston d'Orleans had been Governor of Languedoc.

Page 110. (76) Turenne, the son of the Duc de Bouillon, who was a Sovereign Prince, might be considered as a foreigner. By sending troops to Portugal in the name of Turenne, commanded by Schomberg, likewise a foreign Prince, Louis XIV was not therefore formally violating the Treaty of the Pyrénées.

Page 110. (77) The Portuguese Ambassador to England must be understood.

Page 110. (78) Denmark was emerging from a terrible war with Sweden, from which she had barely escaped being annihilated.

Page 113. (79) Périgny had begun to write *belles ch.*; . . . but these words were afterwards struck out without being replaced.

Page 113. (80) Louis XIV had sent troops under the command of Pradel to help the Dutch against the Bishop of Munster, who was in the pay of the English. In order to avoid a conflict with Spain by forcing a passage through Flanders, the troops had gone by way of the Rhine provinces, who were in alliance with the King, and it was necessary for him to avoid offending them by acts of indiscipline.

Page 115. (81) In his letters, written in February 1666, Louis XIV urged Beaufort to fight the English, and at the same time he wrote to Vivonne " not to be carried away by zeal or courage."

Page 115. (82) The figure remains blank ; previous renderings of the Memoirs of 1666 give : 46 *ships*.

Page 116. (83) The English fleet was commanded by Monck, Duke of Albemarle, and Prince Rupert. This Prince, the son of the Elector Palatine and Elizabeth of England, was first cousin to Charles II and was serving as a general in England. The Dutch fleet was commanded by Ruyter, under whom was Van Tromp. The battle lasted from the 11th to the 14th June 1666.

Page 117. (84) We must remember that this refers to Marie of Savoie, Duchesse de Nemours.

Page 119. (85) Marie Anne of Austria, widow of Philip IV, was acting as Regent during the minority of her son, Charles II, then aged four.

Page 119. (86) He was at that time French Ambassador at Madrid.

Page 121. (87) La Haye Ventelet was the son of the previous Ambassador at Constantinople, who had been imprisoned by the Turks for having refused to pay certain taxes ; whence arose the former tension between the Porte and France.

Page 124. (88) This expedition was made with boldness and endurance by the Marquis de Tracy with 1,200 French soldiers.

Page 124. (89) The Duc de Beaufort in 1665 had vanquished the fleets of Barbary before Tunis and Algiers. On the conclusion of the Treaty, the Pasha of Algiers sent to Louis XIV two lions, an ostrich, and other curiosities.

Page 125. (90) The Infanta Marguerite Thérèse, daughter of Philippe IV, married the Emperor Leopold I in 1666.

Page 126. (91) The Duc d'Enghien, son of the great Condé, married in 1663 Anne of Bavaria, niece of the Queen of Poland ; she brought him as her *dot* the Silesian Duchies of Oppeln and Ratibor.

Page 131. (92) The Languedoc canal was begun at about this time.

Page 132. (93) Here a blank occurs in the manuscript.

Page 134. (94) This refers to the (French) colonies. We shall see further on what happened at St. Christopher, a colony in the Antilles shared by the English and the French.

Page 135. (95) The date is left blank in the manuscript. The encounter took place on 4th August 1666, when the English came out of the Thames. Tromp, driven away and pursued, withdrew, leaving Ruyter engaged with eight ships against twenty-two ; he effected, however, an honourable retreat. Tromp was afterwards dismissed the service.

Page 139. (96) The *Rubis*, which Beaufort decided to send to the bottom. He did not give up, however, until he had discharged all his guns at the English flag-ship.

Page 139. (97) Marie Louise de Gonzague, the wife of John Casimir I. Weary of the unruliness of his subjects, John Casimir was thinking of abdicating in favour of the Duc d'Enghien, his nephew. The Grand Marshal Lubomirsky opposed this project.

Page 144. (98) Charles Emmanuel II had married in 1665 Marie Jeanne de Savoie, daughter of the Duc de Nemours. Her mother, the Duchesse, was Christine of France, the daughter of Henri IV.

Page 145. (99) Alexandre VII nearly died in 1666. Referring to the attitude of his nephews, Louis XIV wrote in his journal : " It is natural for people who are raised up by fortune to be so puffed up as to become ridiculous, and to fall into baseness when it fails them."

Page 145. (100) Four Bishops had refused to sign the formulary (see above, p. 43, note 4). The King presented himself before Parliament to cause an edict to be enrolled putting into execution the Bull condemning the five propositions and ordaining the signature of the formulary.

Page 146. (101) The Corsican guard had insulted Créqui, the French Ambassador, and fired on his coach, killing a page.

Page 146. (102) Louis XIV had not been satisfied at the attitude of the Cardinal over the affair of the Duc de Créqui.

Page 148. (103) Schomberg commanded the French troops in Portugal.

Page 151. (104) Louis XIV was continually thinking of his designs on Flanders.

Page 151. (105) Charles Colbert, Marquis de Croissy.

Page 151. (106) Henrietta of France was then residing in France.

Page 153. (107) The Dutch Plenipotentiary.

Page 154. (108) M. de Saint Aunay, who had retired to Spain in a fit of pique.

Page 156. (109) Bremen had been given to the Swedes by the Westphalia.

Page 156. (110) Otho William, Count of Koenigsmark, was entrusted by Sweden with various embassies. He served afterwards under Turenne, and was created Field-Marshal by Louis XIV. Taking service under Venice, he commanded the troops of the Most Serene Republic in the victorious campaign of the Morea and Athens (1686–

1687). He was the uncle of Philippe de Koenigsmark, celebrated on account of his tragic amours, and of Aurore, famed for her beauty and wit, who was the mistress of Auguste II of Poland, by whom she had a son, who became the Maréchal de Saxe.

Page 157. (111) Christine of Sweden, the daughter of Gustavus Adolphus, had abdicated in 1654. She became a Catholic and retired to Rome. She was celebrated for her love of science and art.

Page 160. (112) The Infanta Catherine of Portugal had brought Tangiers to the King of England as her *dot*.

Page 162. (113) The Marquis of Brandenburg, descended from the last but one Duke of Gueldre, Cleves, Berg, and Juliers, had been a rival of the Duke of Neuburg, who was supported by Spain. In 1666 a composition had been effected : the Duchy of Gueldre continued to form part of the Spanish Low Countries to which it had been annexed in the preceding century ; the Duchies of Berg and Juliers were assigned to the Duke of Neuburg ; and the Marquis of Brandenburg obtained the Duchy of Cleves, which was the beginning of the Prussian power on the Rhine.

Page 163. (114) The musters held on pay days were called *montres*.

Page 166. (115) The *ustensile* was a contribution paid in money by the provinces to the troops stationed in their territory.

Page 169. (116) These pages, the more correct title of which would be : " Reflections on the necessity of inflicting punishment," appear to have been further notes for the continuation of the Memoirs. They were written in 1679 at the moment of Pomponne's disgrace.

Page 170. (117) Hugues de Lionne, who is mentioned in the Memoirs for the year 1661. See above, page 55.

Page 171. (118) Arnauld de Pomponne, Secretary of State for Foreign Affairs from 1671 to 1679, whom we have seen appear several times in the Memoirs as Ambassador to Sweden. He was the brother of the great Arnauld, Arnauld d'Andilly, and of Mère Angélique.

Page 173. (119) A memorandum given by Louis XIV to his grandson, Philippe V, when he was leaving to take possession of the Kingdom of Spain. He was then seventeen years old.

Page 173. (120) The position of this precept between the preceding and the one that follows shows that Louis XIV wished to dissuade Philippe V from amorous *liaisons*.

Page 174. (121) Charles II, who had made the Duc d'Anjou his heir in virtue of the rights of Queen Marie Thérèse.

Page 174. (122) The Marquis of Castel-dos-Rios, Ambassador (Spanish) in Paris, whom Philippe V made a Grandee.

Page 175. (123) French Ambassador at Madrid.

Page 175. (124) Marie Anne de Neuburg, daughter of the Eleɐor Palatine, and the second wife of Charles II, was entirely devoted to Auʃtria, in whose favour she had endeavoured to influence her husband.

Page 175. (125) The Dauphin was ʃtill living; he died in 1711. As the Dauphine was dead, we muʃt here underʃtand by the word " relations " those of the Duc d'Anjou, beginning with the King.

Page 177. (126) This plan of a speech, which is in the handwriting of Louis XIV, seems to have been written in 1710, during the war of the Spanish Succession, at the moment when the *pourparlers* opened at Gertruydenberg were broken off. The allies had laid down conditions which, in spite of the great need for peace, Louis XIV had been unable to accept. They had demanded that he should himself use force to dethrone his grandson.

Page 177. (127) Louis XIV wrote *aʃteure* (*à cette heure*), as was the praɐice of Montaigne.

Page 178. (128) Ibid.

Page 178. (129) Manuscript : " and that we shall be able."